"Beautifully written... perb short introduc... masters of our time...

"The recent pressures of a pandemic, and a dramatic recognition of racism in our age, thankfully impels many of us to respond by undertaking a renewed search for beauty, love, and humility. When this happens, we often turn to a guide that doesn't have the answers but has faced serious questions with a spirit of integrity and wisdom. Thomas Merton, monk, writer, and prophet, is such a person, and Jon Sweeney graciously helps us to meet him. He does this in a way that not only allows us to make his acquaintance but also to then want to go further so he might become our friend in these uncertain times. The simplicity in this book is surprising because so many complex issues and characters who touched Merton's life are introduced. This is a much-needed bridge to reach Merton, or visit him again, so we can sit with the themes of solitude, inner freedom, silence, and respect for all humanity. I am happy this little treasure of a book is present now when we need it most."

—Robert J. Wicks, author of *The Tao of Ordinariness: Humility and Simplicity in a Narcissistic Age*

"If Thomas Merton's life and work amount to something like the Louvre or the Met—full of shimmering masterpieces, weird sketches, and hidden subterranean passageways—Sweeney is the perfect docent to show us around. This indispensable guide to America's most famous monk is both spirited and measured, an insightful examination of a monolithic writer that never veers into hagiography."

—Dan Hornsby, author of *Via Negativa: A Novel*

THOMAS MERTON

ALSO BY JON M. SWEENEY

St. Francis of Assisi: His Life, Teachings, and Practice

A Course in Christian Mysticism, by Thomas Merton (editor)

*The Enthusiast: How the Best Friend of Francis of Assisi
Almost Destroyed What He Started*

Francis of Assisi in His Own Words: The Essential Writings, 2nd ed.
(translator and editor)

*Inventing Hell: Dante, the Bible, and Eternal Torment,
Second Edition,* foreword by Richard Rohr

Meister Eckhart's Book of the Heart: Meditations for the Restless Soul
(with Mark S. Burrows)

*The Pope Who Quit: A True Medieval Tale of Mystery,
Death, and Salvation*

*The Road to Assisi: The Essential Biography of St. Francis,
by Paul Sabatier* (editor)

The St. Clare Prayer Book: Listening for God's Leading

The St. Francis Prayer Book: A Guide to Deepen Your Spiritual Life

*When Saint Francis Saved the Church: How a Converted Medieval
Troubadour Created a Spiritual Vision for the Ages*

Nicholas Black Elk: Medicine Man, Catechist, Saint

THOMAS MERTON

*An
Introduction
to His Life,
Teachings, and
Practices*

———

JON M. SWEENEY

ST. MARTIN'S
ESSENTIALS
NEW YORK

First published in the United States by St. Martin's Essentials,
an imprint of St. Martin's Publishing Group

THOMAS MERTON. Copyright © 2021 by Jon M. Sweeney.
All rights reserved. Printed in the United States of America.
For information, address St. Martin's Publishing Group,
120 Broadway, New York, NY 10271.

www.stmartins.com

The Library of Congress Cataloging-in-Publication
Data is available upon request.

ISBN 978-1-250-25048-3 (trade paperback)
ISBN 978-1-250-25049-0 (ebook)

Our books may be purchased in bulk for promotional, educational,
or business use. Please contact your local bookseller or the Macmillan
Corporate and Premium Sales Department at 1-800-221-7945,
extension 5442, or by email at
MacmillanSpecialMarkets@macmillan.com.

First Edition: 2021

10 9 8 7 6 5 4 3 2 1

For my Trappist friends,
present and gone

Contents

There is in all things an invisible fecundity . . . a hidden wholeness.

—THOMAS MERTON

Simple Chronology

1915   (January 31) Born in Prades, France.

1921   Mother dies, October 3.

1928   Moves in May with father to England, to a suburb of London.

1931   Father dies, January 18, just before Tom's sixteenth birthday.

1933   In spring, reads the Bible like a pilgrim in Rome; in October, enters Clare College, Cambridge.

1934–35 Forced to leave Cambridge in June. Enters Columbia University, New York City, the following January. Remains there five years, earning both BA and MA degrees.

1938   In July, leaves grandparents' home on Long Island for an apartment on West 114th Street, Manhattan. Received into Roman Catholic Church on November 16. Spends the next couple of years with uncertainty, searching for answers and purpose.

1941	In April, Holy Week retreat at Trappist monastery in Kentucky, Our Lady of Gethsemani; on December 10, at twenty-six, enters Gethsemani as a novice.
1944	Sees his first book published: *Thirty Poems*.
1948	His abbot, Dom Frederic Dunne, dies in early August. October 4, *The Seven Storey Mountain* is published. The book is endorsed by Graham Greene, Clare Boothe Luce, Bishop Fulton J. Sheen, and Evelyn Waugh. By Christmas, *Time* magazine and *The New York Times* declare it a bestseller.
1948	Begins contemplating leaving Gethsemani for a religious order or foundation more genial to silence and solitude.
1949	Ordained a priest May 26. Family and literary friends attend the service, among them his editor, Robert Giroux, who mentions that sales of *The Seven Storey Mountain* have reached two hundred thousand copies. On October 6, he writes Merton to say the number has increased to three hundred thousand.
1953	In February, receives his first taste of hermitage, spending days in a converted toolshed in the woods that he called "St. Anne's."
1955	In October, Abbot Dom James asks him to be novice master.
1956	Writes first letter to D. T. Suzuki, Japanese expert on Zen Buddhism, introducing himself as "a monk, a Christian, and so-called contemplative of a rather strict Order. . . . who . . . has a great love of and interest in Zen."[1]

1958	Has his famous epiphany of the oneness of all people on March 18 in downtown Louisville at the corner of 4th and Walnut (now Muhammad Ali Boulevard).
1959	Petitions the Vatican to leave Gethsemani but remain a monk. Request denied.
1961	In July, begins writing *Cold War Letters* and articles on war and peace, sometimes subverting the orders of his religious superiors.
1965	Begins living permanently in his final hermitage starting in August. Then writes a letter, which is never sent, to Pope Paul VI, again requesting a release from his vows, this time to join the contemplative community founded by Fr. Ernesto Cardenal in Nicaragua.
1966	Has brief affair with a young nurse (known as "M"), while in Louisville for medical treatment. This becomes the most serious break of his vows, and a crisis of faith. Also publishes two books showing a deep and urgent engagement with the world's problems.
1968	New abbot is elected at Gethsemani in January. Merton leaves the monastery on September 11, visiting New Mexico, Alaska, and San Francisco, before flying to Asia October 15. Dies December 10 in his room in Bangkok, Thailand, by accidental electrocution after giving a talk at a monastic conference. Several days later, the body is flown to California aboard a military bomber originating in Vietnam. Buried December 17 at the Abbey of Gethsemani.

Introduction

I would love to know what brought you here. What led you to go looking for Thomas Merton? I have my own reasons, which I'll mention in a minute.

He's famous, at least as famous as a monk can be. His autobiography, *The Seven Storey Mountain,* is the bestselling autobiographical book written by a monastic since St. Augustine's *Confessions,* which first appeared in the fifth century. That's a 1,500-year gap between bestsellers. Even today, nearly seventy-five years after *The Seven Storey Mountain* was published, spiritual directors, college professors, campus ministers, vowed religious, and reading groups still actively recommend it. It is a true classic. So is Merton, which can't honestly be said about many religious figures from the twentieth century.

Not long ago, in 2015, Pope Francis recommended Merton in the first speech a pope ever gave before a joint session of the U.S. Congress. Pope Francis named four Americans that day as exemplary: Abraham Lincoln, Martin Luther King Jr., Dorothy

Day, and Thomas Merton. Merton, the pope said, was "above all a man of prayer, a thinker who challenged the certitudes of his time and opened new horizons for souls and for the church. He was also a man of dialogue, a promoter of peace between peoples and religions." Thousands of people that night, including me, live streaming the speech or watching on television, cheered out loud. I'm not exaggerating. I've confirmed this with many friends. Audible cheers were heard outside apartments, condos, and houses throughout the land. How unexpected it was! (More on that later.) At the same time, thousands of others must surely have turned to each other on their couches as the pope mentioned Merton alongside President Lincoln, and said, *Who's that?*

Thomas Merton is the one who wrote, "There is in all things an invisible fecundity . . . a hidden wholeness." He wrote a lot of things (more on that later, too). But this quote is emblematic of his body of work—and his life. Throughout his life, Merton searched for the elusive wholeness that we all know somehow lurks nearby. This is what we all want for our lives—wholeness, integration, vitality, growth. And the opposites of those things are what we very much *don't* want.

It is only by looking to Merton's books that we begin to discover how much his search for spiritual truth was part of his own journey. He chronicled his experiences. He was a writer because it was by writing that he figured out who he was. For these reasons, the best approach to understanding him is to look at his chronological life, and the books, ideas, people, travels, and encounters that defined who he was at each step along the way. That's what we will do here.

We all search for that elusive fecundity and wholeness in our own ways, and as a great spiritual writer, Merton consistently described his search in the most compelling of language. That's what you find in the bestselling books—and we will look at those—and there are many of them. But most of all, this introduction to Merton will be about the search for wholeness itself. I don't want this to be a place where you simply glean information about a famous twentieth-century Christian. I want you to find help on your own way. That is, in fact, what Merton wanted to do with all his writing: help readers find God and themselves, hopefully on paths that converge.

About the search for wholeness, Merton was always certain. And by the end of his life, he may even have found what he was looking for. We'll see. You'll be ready to decide that for yourself before we're done.

HE CONFUSES A LOT OF PEOPLE

"We are all secrets," Merton wrote one day in his private journal. In other words, there are limits to how much we can understand ourselves, let alone each other. Particularly, we can't presume to understand someone else's religious or spiritual life. What is "on the surface" tells only a fraction of their story.

Another twentieth-century favorite of mine is Edith Stein, the Jewish philosopher who converted to Roman Catholicism, became a Carmelite nun, and then died in a Nazi concentration camp. The Nazis didn't care if a Jew had converted to another religion. After her tragic death, Stein became a saint in the estimation of the Catholic Church, whereas I'm sure Merton never will receive such an honor. (More on that later.) She's officially known in the church as St. Teresa Benedicta of the Cross. Still, her niece once asked her about her conversion to Catholicism from Judaism, and Edith responded with a Latin phrase: *"Secretum meum mihi."* "My secret is mine."

I think you'll find that this is very true of Merton, as well, before you're done reading about his life, writings, and spiritual practices. Our secrets are our own, particularly when it comes to who we are in our relationship with a God who, when communicating with us, if at all, often does so in a whisper.

This is one way of suggesting that we'll never fully understand our subject. It is also a way of saying that Merton's willingness to consistently and consciously be on pilgrimage, to talk with us while he's searching for what he's looking for, and to acknowledge that the search never stops in this life—that the answers are not often clear or simple—makes him an evergreen teacher of spiritual wisdom.

Popularly understood, he was a contemplative monk who introduced the possibility of a deep religious and spiritual life—something one might imagine exists only in a monastery—as available to anyone, whether they lived in a cloister or a city, were Christian or some other religious tradition, and whether or not they felt certain in their beliefs. His own life was full of contradictions, as we will soon see, and it is these very contradictions that also make him appealing to us still. He seems to have found a real and deep personal connection to the living God, and yet some of his actions reveal how very human he remained. Yet that core understanding—that a monastic sort of life might be available to you wherever you live—remains compelling.

Given that he was a monk, it is a wonder that we even know his name. He entered a strict monastery at the age of twenty-six, saying that he was no longer going to be a writer, that writing was mostly about ego, and that as a monk he was instead going to be a person of asceticism and prayer. If things had gone for him the way they went for 99.9 percent of the monks before him, Merton would have prayed and practiced his penance earnestly and quietly, and then died in blissful obscurity. That's the way of most cloistered monks.

But before he turned thirty-five, he wrote one of the best-selling autobiographies ever published—the one I mentioned already—titled *The Seven Storey Mountain*. The first edition of that book, in its original binding and dust jacket, will cost you about $7,500 the last time I checked. It is valuable today as a collector's item because the publisher did not print many of them. Who knew that such a book would be the bestselling non-fiction book in the United States that year? The original publisher, Harcourt Brace, also got in trouble for one of the captions to one of the photographs on the back cover. It showed a group of monks working in the fields, as Trappist monks in Kentucky once did, and although none of the faces of those monks were visible in the photo, the caption read, "Author is second from the left." Merton had joined a religious order in which he was supposedly going to go through life with anonymity.

So why did he write an autobiography in the first place? What happened to the life of quiet prayer to which he'd dedicated himself? This is one of the fascinating stories of Merton's life to be told in the chapters to come. He prayed aplenty, but he also went on to write many, many bestselling books, turning him into a star.

Like many of the great spiritual teachers in every religious tradition, the story of his life is intertwined with his writings. In them, he was always advocating for the spiritual life: encouraging his readers to find and deepen theirs. Dialogue, wonder, paradox, friendship, pilgrimage, and conversation were among his most essential spiritual practices. These teachings are what still draw many seekers to him.

But as I hope to show you, I believe that his chief vocation—which he finally accepted for himself late in life—was as a writer. Writing was how he entered the world. It was how he understood the world and found his place in it. It is also his best way to show others how they may find their own places and paths today, and Merton remains enormously popular among spiritual seekers for this reason. They discover his books in their own quests. They also find their quests echoed in the pages of his books. One such person is Fr. James Martin, SJ, popular Catholic author and former corporate executive turned Jesuit priest. Fr. Martin says:

Thomas Merton's writings were one of the main reasons I left a job at General Electric and entered the Jesuit order in the late 1980s. A chance encounter with a television documentary on his life led me to track down and read The Seven Storey Mountain. *But it was this quote, from* No Man Is an Island, *that stopped me dead in my tracks as an aspiring corporate executive: "Why do we have to spend our lives striving to be something that we would never want to be, if we only knew what we wanted? Why do we waste our time doing things which, if we only stopped to think about them, are just the opposite of what we were made for?*"[1]

For all these reasons, it is no wonder that *many* of Merton's books were autobiographies, memoirs, and personal journals. He discovered spiritual insight in the context of living. He worked on his spiritual practices while exploring the meaning in his life and doings. He couldn't shake off where he'd come from, and he didn't want to. He was like the author of the other greatest autobiography in English in the twentieth century, Stephen Spender, who once said: "Autobiography provides the line of continuity in my work. I am not someone who can shed or disclaim his past."[2] For these reasons, the structure of this book follows the basic chronological trajectory of Merton's life, with occasional flashes forward and flashbacks, and his teachings and practices are woven throughout.

I love his vision—you get a sense of it in every paragraph—and his eyes: what they saw. He never stopped looking. He was ever curious. In his last decade, that looking and curiosity extended to photography and drawing, as well. His gaze moved outward toward others, to the created world, and to inanimate objects like old barns and railroad tracks, captured in black-and-white photographs. Such images—and they've been published before (see the "Suggestions for Further Reading" at the back of this book)—were a mirror of what he was seeing inside himself. Similarly, his drawings were usually with a black pen or brush, on clean white paper. He did self-portraits, Zen images, and simple figures. There's clear joy in them. Early in his conversion,

Merton was looking at and writing about things like personal sin, repentance, and turning away from the world. In his final decade, he was looking more often at opportunity, open fields, new and different and more expansive paths, and congruent shapes; one gets the sense that he eventually came to see the inability to see opportunity and change itself as a kind of sin.

That quotation from Merton repeated by James Martin, SJ, is worth repeating: "Why do we have to spend our lives striving to be something that we would never want to be, if we only knew what we wanted? Why do we waste our time doing things which, if we only stopped to think about them, are just the opposite of what we were made for?"[3] Merton inspires. He gave his books titles like *Zen and the Birds of Appetite* and *The Wisdom of the Desert*. Merton is not your usual Catholic priest, monk, or writer.

I also love his smile and his hands—these things we came to know in the decades following that initial bestselling autobiography in which the publisher was reprimanded for pointing out the author in a blurry photograph. Times changed, and quickly, and within just a few years, the monk-writer who shouldn't be identified became an international figure.

If he had been a monk of the Middle Ages, we wouldn't know his smile and his hands, but Merton was very much a man of the second half of the twentieth century, and he was photographed with a variety of other writers, religious figures, and famous people. You can find photos of Merton, for instance, with the Dalai Lama, Thich Nhat Hanh, Joan Baez, Wendell Berry, and Daniel Berrigan, SJ.

To see him, you'd think perhaps he was a sculptor or a high

school football coach. He was of average height and a sturdy build. He had strong hands. At times, wearing glasses and bent over a book, he appeared to be an intellectual. At other times, the smile on his shining face reflected the playfulness that filled him. That smile and those hands brought him close friendships with people of every religious tradition, every fascinating thinker, every poet, and even local Kentucky farmers who wanted some interesting conversation after the sun went down. To see Merton's own photographs—because he took many—is to understand more of who he was, and again, that extraordinary vision.

He had written so many books by the time he turned fifty that words began to feel noisy to him. The photography offered another way of speaking, seeing, and gesturing. For him, it was both a new way of "articulating the silence" of his life, and an "antidote to the noisiness of the world."[4]

"Those who love their life lose it, and those who hate their life in this world will keep it for eternal life." This, from the Gospel of St. John, chapter 12, is one of the most popular scripture texts read in Catholic funeral liturgies. There are great mysteries in that short verse. One could argue that Thomas Merton embraced it but also that he spent his life overturning it.

WHY ANOTHER BOOK ABOUT HIM?

There are so many books about Merton, so why another?

I can only offer this, by way of explanation: I think that this one does something a little differently, by taking a look at his life, teachings, and practices all together, and in a way that speaks directly to religiously unanchored people living in the twenty-first century.

We will begin with his death, in 1968, and then go back in time to better see his beginnings and who and how he had become. Who Merton was at the end of his life was an evolved spiritual creature unlike the one who stepped into the monastery in Kentucky for the first time twenty-seven years earlier. I don't think we can know him in a way that's relevant for our own spiritual seeking and finding the way without starting (rather than ending) with who he was at the end of his life. He had come to a point of understanding love in profound ways, embracing strangers and the unfamiliar with courage and abandon, and discovering truth in the spiritualities of the East in ways that forever changed his own faith tradition.

Another of his famous teachings centered around discovering to differentiate between our "true selves" and our "false selves." Like most teachers and their teachings, he didn't invent this one but discovered it in the monastic tradition of which he was a part (called Cistercian; Trappist is a branch of Cistercian). This will come up again later, but in essence, Merton was passionately convinced that every person has a unique version for being like Christ in the world, and we can't discover this for ourselves without a lot of prayer and help from God, without complete self-honesty, and without undoing all the ways that we've learned to hide behind falsity. We find, discover, and become our true selves. We become godly.

If you've read anything previously about this unique twentieth-century religious figure, you've probably heard that he was important for bringing the spiritual practices and wisdom teachings of the monastery to people on the outside of monastery walls. He gave us access. Merton showed those of us who aren't monks—and won't ever be monks—how to be like one. I was moved by that emphasis in understanding Merton's legacy when I was younger.

WHAT BROUGHT ME HERE

I was only a year old when Merton died. But when I was seventeen and contemplating having to register with selective service as eligible for the draft, I had a feeling that I shouldn't be willing to kill others, even in a war. I didn't find people who were friendly to objecting to military service in my church, but someone pointed me to a Mennonite nonprofit nearby, and I met with the director there. It was he who first put a Thomas Merton book in my hands: a collection of Merton's writings on peace. Then, when I was nineteen, after having devoured *The Seven Storey Mountain*'s five hundred or so pages in three days of excited reading, I made the first of several visits to Merton's monastery in Kentucky, pondering a monastic life. Should I? Eventually, I decided no. Instead, I would try to be what is sometimes called a "monk in the world." I became a disciple of the teachings of those who emphasized the contemplative aspect of the spiritual life.

Today, there are far fewer monks left at the Abbey of Gethsemani than there were when Merton was alive. Hundreds of monks lived there at one time, some sixty or seventy years ago. Today, they are perhaps a few dozen. Organized religious life is on the wane everywhere you look, and monastery populations are no exception. The population of every monastic community has been aging every year for decades. Some monasteries have closed. Others survive only because they have become places of retreat, as people like you and me visit for a weekend or two a year. Also, many monasteries have a large numbers of oblates, or associates—laypeople who commit to living with monastic rhythms and spiritual practices, and financially support the monastery. I suspect that Merton could see that this would one day be the case. (See the start of the next chapter.)

Those of us who visit monasteries on retreat, and who pursue the spiritual practices of someone like Thomas Merton, are indeed among the keepers of the monastic way. We don't—we can't—do it like he did. But in many ways, we can be monks, and I hope you find your own way as you read this book.

Not long ago at the Abbey of Gethsemani, I spent an afternoon with one of the monks and a friend at Merton's old hermitage in the woods. Although there is a right way to see this special place—by permission, without trespassing—it also isn't uncommon for people to make their way to the hermitage in their own way, and the monks are generally gracious and forgiving about it. In fact, the trespassing has been happening since Merton's own lifetime; he spent a fair amount of time ducking people in the woods who were trying to find "that famous monk."

Merton liked to walk in the predawn hours as the mist was rising, observing wrens, cardinals, woodpeckers, and the occasional mockingbird along the way. On this particular morning not long ago, as my two companions and I were walking from the hermitage back to the abbey, I spied a folded single sheet of paper soaking on the grass in the morning dew. I bent down and picked it up.

Someone had printed out a Merton poem and carried it with them, probably to read it while sitting on the hermitage porch the night before. It had fallen out of the pocket, quite recently, of someone who had walked back down the same hill we were walking down. "His God lives in his emptiness like an affliction," is one of the lines from the poem on that paper soaking in the dew. The poem is titled "When in the Soul of the Serene Disciple." It was that emptiness, but also the knowing that God was there in it, that moved Merton throughout his life.

I tucked the poem in my pocket as we all walked down the hill in the woods, then crossed the road, toward where the gate used to stand that Merton was so happy had once enclosed him inside, about eighty years before.

THOMAS MERTON

1

He's Finally Free

"We cannot rely on structures," Merton said in the final talk he gave. He was in Bangkok, Thailand, for a conference of monastics of Eastern and Western religious traditions. They were there to share spiritual practices and discuss concerns about where the world was headed. As monks and nuns, what could they do to help, and how should they relate to a turbulent world?

It was 1968, one of the terrible years of the terrible twentieth century. The United States was mired in an unwinnable and increasingly immoral war in Southeast Asia. It was in 1968 that that famous photograph was taken of a Viet Cong officer being summarily executed on the street by a South Vietnamese national police chief. You may remember it: Nguyễn Văn Lém shot point-blank in the right temple by Nguyễn Ngọc Loan. That photo appeared in newspapers across the globe and won the Pulitzer Prize a year later. Presidential candidate Robert Kennedy, upon whom so many hopes had been placed, had also been killed by an assassin's bullet in 1968, in Los Angeles. And

Martin Luther King Jr. was murdered by a man who objected to a vision for the future that focused on justice, equal rights, and inclusion. That spring and summer, the world also watched as Czechoslovakians started a revolution against Soviet rule, only to be put down violently by their oppressors in August.

Merton was in Bangkok having just spent eight exhilarating weeks visiting friends and experiencing firsthand many of the Taoist, Hindu, and Buddhist temples and locations that he'd been studying from Kentucky for a decade. Calcutta, New Delhi, the Himalayas, Madras, Ceylon (Sri Lanka), and then Bangkok. He was discovering what he'd seen only in books, and he was finding both ancient and new things inside himself. One might also say he was taking a much-needed break from being immersed in world events. He was exhausted from constant work at his typewriter, from feeling the weight on his shoulders of thousands of activists for justice and peace who relied on his regular wisdom.

The journal he kept on his weeks of pilgrimage in Asia will be one of the many sources I refer to in the course of these pages. It is called *The Asian Journal* and was pulled together by Merton's three closest literary friends from the notebooks, journals, and clippings that the monk kept while he was away from home. All of Merton's journals, in fact, and his letters, are the most valuable glimpses we have into his personality, his friendships, and how he understood his vocation.

He was among old and new friends when he got up to give that final talk in Bangkok. He was more "Fr. Louis" (that was his monastic name) there than he was the famous author, Thomas

Merton. In his talk, he addressed what he called his own "identity crisis" as a monk who was trying to find "how he identifies himself in a world of revolution." He spoke as one who was not so much interested in changing the structures of the world as he was interested in changing the consciousness of people: what is inside of them. He spoke as the contemplative that he was.

Something he said in the middle of that lecture went mostly unremarked upon that day and in the days and months after his death. You see—his death took place, by freak accident, that very evening after he returned to his room. He was electrocuted, apparently after touching a fan with faulty wiring soon after emerging wet from the bathtub. But I think what he said that afternoon that was missed reveals the heart of a man who had journeyed bleary-eyed around the world, from a lonely childhood in Europe, to a dissolute life at university in England, to a literary life in New York City, to a cloister in Kentucky, to the mountains of India and Nepal, and then to a podium in Thailand.

He was weary. He was done. He wasn't even sure that he would make it home. And he felt that he stood mostly alone. He said:

We can no longer rely on being supported by structures that may be destroyed at any moment by a political power or a political force. You cannot rely on structures. The time for relying on structures has disappeared. They are good and they should help us, and we should do the best we can with them. But they may be taken away, and if everything is taken away, what do you do next?[1]

By strange irony, Merton's body was carried back to the United States on a plane full of Vietnam War American soldier casualties. Fenton Johnson, the Kentucky novelist and essayist who grew up a stone's throw from the Abbey of Gethsemani, in Kentucky, once recalled in an essay for *The Atlantic,* "Merton the pacifist mystic monk in his shiny black body bag amid a hundred and more dead soldiers in their shiny black body bags—an image of solitude amid unity if ever one was known." Johnson, who grew up knowing dozens of the monks who knew Merton well, went on: "As my mother tells it, the coroner called in my father, together with several monks, to identify the body, but after more than a week in a tropical country it was too decomposed to identify except by its false teeth, which Merton's Lexington dentist recognized, and which are still, or so my mother believes, in his possession."[2]

Not many monks have an obituary on the front page of *The New York Times,* as Merton did. THOMAS MERTON IS DEAD AT 53; MONK WROTE OF SEARCH FOR GOD, the headline read beside a smiling photograph of him. I imagine that Thich Nhat Hanh and H. H. the Dalai Lama will also be so honored—and that's the company Merton keeps.

Monastic rules and walls and bells could only take him so far, the famous monk had come to realize. Ultimately, these things had little to do, he had learned firsthand, with real inner transformation. By the time he died, he was truly free.

2

A World-Weary Man

His mother called him Tom. He was born to artist parents in January 1915. Father, Owen, was Kiwi; mother, Ruth, was American, from Ohio. His place of birth was Prades, a small town in the French Pyrenees, close to the border with Spain, along one of the primary pilgrim roads to Santiago de Compostela ("The Camino"). He was baptized into the Church of England, his father's tradition.

World War I was underway throughout the European continent at that time. German troops had already invaded France and Belgium, and Great Britain had declared war on Germany. The famous Christmas Day Truce was real: men on the western front of both sides emerged from their trenches to bury the dead, smoke cigarettes, and even play impromptu soccer matches. But it wouldn't even last a week.

Nevertheless, Prades was an out-of-the-way place in the mountains. It took another eighteen months before German troops advanced near the place of Merton's birth, where Tom's father was struggling to make a name for himself as a painter. Then, the fighting forced the family to leave for the United States. They went to live with Ruth's parents on Long Island. Two years later, they were still in New York but living in a small rented house of their own. Then Ruth gave birth to another boy, Tom's brother, John Paul. Three years after that, Ruth died from cancer. Tom was not allowed to see his mother in the hospital (Bellevue, in New York City). The family wanted to shield him from the visual of seeing her in such a state. We know better now—how important it is, even for a child, to be able to say goodbye. His mother wrote him a letter to say that she was soon going to die and that they would never see each other again.

LIFE WITH FATHER

These early years were filled with confusion, pain, and transience. Is it any wonder that later he would seek permanence and stability so earnestly? With Tom's mother dead, his father left him alone, first for two years in the company of his maternal grandparents in Douglaston—a city on the north shore of Long Island. Tom enjoyed his time there and remembered fondly visiting his pop at his office at Grosset and Dunlap Publishers in Manhattan. Pop was a book publisher. Owen was away in France, being an artist.

Then Owen returned, convinced that he wanted to take both of his boys back to France with him. He'd first take Tom, and while Tom attended school, Owen would build a house. Soon, Tom was again in the confused environment of Europe, this time just after the First World War had ended, enrolled in school in Saint-Antonin-Noble-Val, in the Occitanie region of south-central France. The war had left Western civilization in shatters. It brought about a dissolution of the old order and a recognition that there is perhaps no real order at all.

Tom was ten when he arrived in Saint-Antonin-Noble-Val. Rural France was a land in its people and culture and architecture largely unchanged since the time of the late medieval Crusades. Merton's mind would hold on to the images he saw in those places and then return to them in his memory when he first visited the Abbey of Gethsemani decades later. He understood that part of the appeal of the monastery was probably because he had, at such an early age, admired similar places on journeys with his father. From his dad, he gained an appreciation for the aesthetics of churches. They visited many on their travels around the French countryside.

Tom was eleven when his father sent him forty kilometers away to board at a lycée (secondary school) in nearby Montauban. He felt very alone at school, away from everyone and everything he knew—most of all, his father. Appreciating aesthetics would come back to him, later, as memory. Now he was lonely. He turned to precocity—the sort that one associates with young would-be intellectuals at lycée. How many twelve-year-olds, for instance, start writing novels? Alone again, Tom did.

In the spring of 1928, two and a half years after they'd arrived together in France, Owen announced to Tom that they were moving again, this time to England. Tom was pleased at this prospect. Now fourteen, he began to show more than precocity; the early signs of his brilliance are traced back to the time he spent at Oakham School, the secondary school in the East Midlands (about two hours north of London) where Owen enrolled his son.

Tom turned fifteen at Oakham during his first year there. He was winning prizes for his schoolwork, beginning to stand out from the other students. Then, his father died in a London hospital of a brain tumor in January 1931, just before Tom's sixteenth birthday. Merton would later remember how he felt then: "I became a true citizen of my own disgusting century: the century of poison gas and atomic bombs."[1] Owen's attending physician, Tom Bennett, was an old friend of Owen's from New Zealand. He'd also been named Tom's godfather at his baptism. Bennett became the legal guardian to Owen's now-orphaned son.

His whole life, Thomas Merton would retain the feeling of being an orphan, of being alone, of being passed around from place to place, guardian to guardian, "treated as a thing," he once wrote, "and not as a person."[2]

COLLEGE CONFUSION

At eighteen, with the equivalent of high school completed, his guardian paid for Tom to spend a late winter month on the European continent. It was a graduation present. He stayed several days in France, mostly in and around Marseilles, often walking, hitchhiking, making friends, and recording his experiences in the manner one came to associate with the beatniks two decades later. What an interesting voice he must have had then: a bit of the French countryside artist, and some would-be London intellectual, tinged with that irreplaceable American overconfidence. Then he took a train to Genoa and down into Italy, from Florence down to Rome.

In Rome, traveling alone, while discovering the art and culture and history, Tom reads the Bible for the first time. Like "a pilgrim," as he tells it, in *The Seven Storey Mountain.* He also begins to consider his life in spiritual and religious terms for the first time. We have only how he describes this a decade later, but still, it is telling:

> *I saw and my whole being rose up in revolt against what was within me, and my soul desired escape. . . . And now I think for the first time in my whole life I really began to pray.*[3]

This temptation and impulse to escape would return to him again and again in his life. Soon, however, Tom was back in metropolitan New York City for the summer, forgetting all this, and then back to England to become a student at Cambridge University. Awakening within forgotten.

Having shone at Oakham, learning the classics, excelling at both ancient and modern languages, he had earned a scholarship to Clare College, Cambridge. Merton was wounded by his father's death and his own loneliness in ways that he couldn't handle or yet understand. Soon, he was getting into trouble at school, living a life that's predictable of a college student, but dissipated nonetheless. He left Cambridge at the end of that first school year, having gotten a young woman pregnant. His guardian, Tom Bennett, was fed up, and essentially sent Tom home to his grandparents in New York for them to deal with him. Tom would later write, kindly, about Tom Bennett: "He . . . gave me credit for being more intelligent and mature than I was, and this of course pleased me very much."[4]

Merton made the most of his modest humiliation, with the opportunity to start over. (He was already quite experienced at starting over, at the young age of nineteen.) Transferring to Columbia University in New York, he "landed on his feet," starting there in January 1935, and living at home at his grandparents' place on Long Island. While some of the college frivolities continued, there was also some serious study and tutelage under key professors that would become formative for his thinking and his soul. The first year it was Mark Van Doren, the poet and critic who was then early in his career in the English Department. By senior year, it was Daniel Walsh, who was only adjunct at Columbia, but whose seminar on Thomas Aquinas opened Tom's eyes for the first time to theology and philosophy. Both were brilliant men and devout Catholics. It was Walsh who would later suggest, in a conversation they had at a bar, that Tom check out the Trappists. That sense of conversion, which had begun more than a year earlier on that solitary trip to Rome, was again beginning to stir in Tom.

He was five feet nine inches tall, of medium build, with a big and easy smile. He made friends easily. One of those friends said, "In terms of sophistication, he was miles ahead of most of us. . . . He did all the things we thought about but didn't do—at least, not yet. He drank a lot, partied, chased (and caught) women. He impressed the hell out of . . . us by saying he had learned Hungarian in bed. Beyond these classical youthful, gallant boasts, he was also a very serious man."[5]

Tom spent his free time editing the school yearbook, dis-covering jazz—live in clubs, this was when the swing era was just starting—and developing friendships with other Columbia writers and artists such as Robert Lax, the poet, and Bob Gi-roux, the publisher. In 1936, the jazz scene in New York City included Louis Armstrong and his orchestra, Lionel Hampton in the Benny Goodman Quartet, and a twenty-one-year-old Billie Holiday already making a name for herself. Tom wanted to ex-perience it all.

But, emotionally, he remained immature—worldly wise but still very young. One of the most poignant passages of his auto-biography is one in which he tells of looking down from a hotel window, into Times Square, imagining what it would feel like to jump. He was confused—a university student who had seen more of the world—the post–First World War world of the 1920s and early '30s in which people felt that every certainty, security, and sense of enchantment had not so much ebbed away as it had been abruptly shattered. Men and women everywhere were seeking meaning in the vacuums of what used to exist.

He flirted briefly with Communism while a student at Co-lumbia. This shouldn't shock us so much today. We should re-member how, at that time, Adolf Hitler was rising to power in Germany and Benito Mussolini was establishing secret police and outlawing labor strikes in Italy. Both were threatening the stability of Europe and the world, and many good and thought-ful people were considering Communism as the most viable po-litical alternative to combat the rise of Fascism. Not to mention the fact that Americans at that time saw themselves on the same side as Russia in what would become the Second World War.

It wasn't yet understood how terribly wrong the Communist system played out in real life. Still, Tom was not very serious about politics of any kind during these years. He was mostly restless, shifting easily from one thing to another.

It is interesting that he lived with his grandparents on Long Island for three years while at Columbia. For such a "man on the town," he was usually sleeping back at home. But in the summer of 1938, he moved to an apartment on West 114th Street, adjacent to the Columbia campus. It is probably no accident that, having moved physically away from the family Protestantism, we then see Tom rapidly immerse himself in Catholic life, both publicly and privately, from his Manhattan apartment.

He began going to mass at Corpus Christi Catholic Church on West 121st Street. He began to pray privately, in church, and at home. He discovered the poetry of the Jesuit Gerard Manley Hopkins. A Hindu monk, Mahanambrata Brahmachari, ten years his senior, set the questing Merton, along with his friend Robert Lax, on a course of reading Catholic classics. Reconnect with your religious roots, the yogi told Merton, then, who was expecting instead guidance in devotion to Vishnu. Then, in September 1938, while reading about Hopkins seeking the help of churchman John Henry Newman (now "St. John Henry Newman"), as Hopkins was considering converting, Merton decided to seek out the priest at Corpus Christi in Manhattan. There, and with that priest, Merton studied the Catholic catechism. And on November 16, 1938, Merton was baptized at Corpus Christi, receiving Communion for the first time that day.

SEEKING A VOCATION

Post-conversion, now a Catholic, living in Greenwich Village, spending summers and occasional weekends with friends at a cabin upstate in Olean, New York, Merton was still finding his way. Purpose had filled him, but it took a while for his occupations to catch up. He tried to discern his vocation, and the restlessness continued. Should he try becoming a Jesuit? Gerard Manley Hopkins—the nineteenth-century poet whom Tom admired—had become a Jesuit, and Tom had begun attending a Jesuit parish in the Village. But that idea was rejected for being too "active" and too "military" in feel.[6] Then, when Tom asked his Corpus Christi priest for guidance, it was suggested he might become a priest in a parish, unattached to a religious order—a so-called secular priest. Given his response to the Jesuit notion, you might think that a secular priest would be more congenial to his tastes, but not so. There was a seriousness to Merton that leaned him toward the vows of a religious order. Call it the face of the convert, but his old friend Robert Lax says it was much more than that: "[T]here was this other aspect of him that was always there and had always been there," Lax said.[7] He turned to the Franciscans first, and soon he was waiting to hear from them about an application to become a friar.

But he was never single-minded. He was also shopping a novel around to various publishers at that time. *My Argument with the Gestapo* would only be published in 1968, after Merton's death.

Then, the Second World War was underway in Europe. (In fact, *My Argument with the Gestapo* told the story of a young man traveling from the United States to Europe when Germany was making war.) President Franklin D. Roosevelt was trying to avoid bringing the United States into the conflict, and every man of draft age was following the headlines with a sense of personal anxiety. Tom was prepared to declare himself a conscientious objector, if it came to that. Meanwhile, despite his new faith and religious life, many of his dissipating ways of living continued.

Then came another turning point. By Christmas 1939—we know, from the journal he kept then—drinking, movies, jazz clubs, and socializing with friends began to go cold for him. Teaching at Columbia was his only real joy left, and the desire to be published. He was an intellectual who wanted to be heard, and that desire was pitted in his imagination against a more burning desire for monastic life, which meant to be quieted. Which would it be for him?

Thrown into this complicated mix, which is ripe for some psychological analysis, was his sense of failure and resignation. In a February 1940 letter to friend Robert Lax, he says: "The more I think about all the stuff I have written the less I care, because the more I know it is junk. Notwithstanding I send you a pome [poem]."[8] So the inner conflict went on.

DESPAIR AND MOMENTUM

When the Franciscans said no to his application to become a friar, he despaired further. What would he do now? There was at least one day, perhaps more, in July 1940 when he was in tears after hearing the bad news from a Franciscan priest in New York. Tom had discussed the possibilities of religious life with him at length, and now he was told that he couldn't enter the novitiate, that his application was being rejected. This happened only after Tom had scrupulously confessed all his past sins—including fathering a child out of wedlock while at Cambridge.

The appeal of monastic life only then grew in him deeper, and he began to turn to even greater strictures that might be imposed upon him for his own good.

To the average outsider, Franciscans and Trappists are both religious orders that demand obedience, poverty, and celibacy, unthinkable commitments, whether we're Catholic or not. But the Franciscans were the Coast Guard of vowed religious life compared to the Trappists, who were the Marines. On the suggestion of his friend and professor from Columbia, Dan Walsh, Merton decided to spend Holy Week 1941 at the Abbey of Gethsemani, home to one of the select houses of silence-practicing, severely ascetical Trappist monks, in Kentucky. (Walsh would follow Merton to Gethsemani, several years later, living with the monks while teaching them philosophy, then moving to a teaching position in nearby Louisville at Bellarmine College.)

Traveling to the middle of the country—a place he had never been, and probably never wanted to go—might have been part of the appeal for Merton. It was new. Perhaps the location in Kentucky was even a kind of penance. He wrote of that first spiritual retreat at the Abbey, "[O]ver all the valley smiled the mild, gentle Easter moon, the full moon, in her kindness, loving this silent place."[9] This was something no one he knew had ever even tried, and when he returned to New York City or upstate to the Olean cabin with his friends, he didn't discuss it much.

That initial Holy Week retreat was in April 1941. A few months later, that fall, Merton was teaching English literature, grammar, and writing to students at St. Bonaventure College, also in Olean. He knew the situation was only temporary. St. Bonaventure was a Franciscan college, and the Franciscans had rejected him. He also began writing another failed novel then. And he spent time volunteering to work among the poor in Harlem at Friendship House, which had been founded by Baroness Catherine de Hueck Doherty, the famous Russian philanthropist and Catholic social activist whom he met when she visited campus that summer. De Hueck was impressed by Merton and asked him to come to Harlem to stay. She told him that working among the poor was the vocation he was looking for. He was ripe for such suggestions. For a brief time, he agreed with her. He was torn. He spent weeks pondering the differences between the "active" and "contemplative" life. What is a Christian to do? What was he to do? Perhaps this was the answer for his life.

Then another old friend from Columbia, Professor Mark Van Doren, asked Merton if he was still considering the priesthood. Hadn't he heard that the priesthood wasn't for him, when the Franciscans said no? Van Doren encouraged him to think and pray about it some more. Surely there were other ways to go about it, he suggested. Merton had loved those days in Kentucky in April. So he wrote the monks to ask if he could come again, this time for a long Advent and Christmas stay.

He was delighted when they responded yes.

Quickly, then, he began to imagine this second retreat as more than just a retreat—perhaps it could be the beginning of a complete change in his situation. An answer. Perhaps this was the entrance to the rest of his life, and to the vocation, that he'd been searching for. He made plans to go to Kentucky in late December, as soon as the fall term was ended. Then a letter came from the draft board.

Even before the Japanese carried out their surprise attack on Pearl Harbor in Hawaii on December 7, it had become a nearly foregone conclusion that the United States would enter the war. There were reports that the Japanese navy and armed forces were rapidly making their way across Southeast Asia. The Germans were attacking Moscow (the Soviet Union was on the side of the Allies). And conscription in England now included every able-bodied man between the ages of eighteen and fifty. So, the trip that Merton had intended for Christmas vacation became a more urgent matter. If he were to become a monk and a priest, it was important for him to make that decision sooner than later. So he gave away to his friends anything that he couldn't easily carry in a trunk, and he left for Kentucky in the early morning on December 9.

To grasp the decision that he had made, try to imagine that you have determined, as a New Year's resolution, to stop entirely from reading the daily news. Then you decide to stop all shopping, with the exception of what's absolutely necessary for your daily food and drink, and perhaps a piece of clothing or shoes, but only if and when something has worn out. Then you cease visiting with your friends. You stop going places, seeing people, and attending events or entertainments of any kind. You even stop talking, which discourages friends from visiting and makes it nearly impossible to make new ones. This is essentially what Merton intended to do when he arrived at the Abbey of Gethsemani on December 10, 1941, saying goodbye to his assistant professorship at St. Bonaventure College in Olean, to his friends, to his present and future in the world. He was hoping to remain at Gethsemani for the rest of his life. That's pretty much what he would do.

Next, imagine where your mind would go, without all those ordinary things in your life. Imagine how stir-crazy you would probably feel at first. Then how liberated you might feel at other times. What might you experience, see, or hear that you never knew was possible to experience, see, or hear?

It was a convincing argument that had moved him into Catholicism, but not one based primarily on premises or propositions. For people like Merton, a religious conversion is mostly about a way of seeing—or glimpsing something—that explains the world and their place in it. An earlier mystic, St. John Henry Newman (the one who'd counseled Gerard Manley Hopkins), wrote, "Faith ever [meaning 'always'] begins with a venture, and is rewarded with sight." That gets at what was happening in Merton's life as he walked into the monastery that day. He was rewarded with sight and began to see what had previously been obscured from his vision. But he wouldn't know where it would take him for a few more years to come.

3

Finding What He Was Looking For

As the material objects of religion fade from view, as they have for the last half century in nearly every respect, so does our understanding of religion itself. There is no way to "see" Thomas Merton without seeing the objects of monasticism.

Cowls, with hoods. The covered walk of a cloister, where men with hoods drawn closely over their heads walk in contemplative silence. Men practicing a strange kind of sign language to each other. Iron gates.

The weary and confused Merton found what he had been looking for behind the gates of that Trappist monastery in rural Kentucky. He was able to put his traveling case in a closet, seemingly, for good.

This quotation from his autobiography is one of the most popular Merton quotes of all:

> So Brother Matthew locked the gate behind me and I was enclosed in the four walls of my new freedom.[1]

Those lines appeared on the first page of the final chapter of the 423-page book that will always be Merton's most renowned work: *The Seven Storey Mountain.* It was as if, now locked behind that gate, his wandering soul could settle into the soil and take root. At the same time, he almost seems to know—by using the word *new*—that this freedom was somehow provisional. There would be many threats to this new freedom, in the form of noise, culture, busyness, pride, and phoniness. Years later, Merton would teach the novices at the monastery the lessons of the Desert Fathers, and he would say: "Christ going out into the desert is the model of monastic renunciation. The monk, like Christ, goes into the desert to engage in combat with the spiritual enemy. He must not take anything of the world with him."[2]

Before the famous autobiography was published, Merton's life in the monastery was largely unremarkable, just as it should have been. As Sylvia Townsend Warner writes in *The Corner That Held Them,* her novel about a convent in fourteenth-century France, "A good convent should have no history." This is true of a good monastery, too. And the Abbey of Gethsemani was, in 1941, pretty much the same as was any Cistercian monastery or convent in France in the Middle Ages. The changes in their sort of monastic life were extremely minute between 1400 and 1940.

During those early years, Merton did some work for the abbot, who quickly recognized the young convert's talents, translating books from French and writing about the monastery itself. He also studied for the priesthood. He worked in the fields with the other monks, prayed beside them in choir all day long, and

slept dormitory-style. There was no escaping the community nature of monastic life.

Praying in choir must have been both exciting and jarring.
Every monk's day began at 2:00 a.m. when bells woke them and
they all quickly made their way to the abbey church for prayers
known as Matins. The word *Matins,* from Middle English, means
"morning," which is a bit ironic given the time of day. In the Old
Testament, the book of Lamentations includes this—

Arise, cry out in the night, at the beginning of the watches!
Pour out your heart like water before the presence of the Lord!
(2:19)

—and that is how it felt, and feels, when praying Matins in the
middle of the night in a cold stone monastery church.

After this, there was time for personal prayer or reading, or
returning briefly to sleep while the priests in the community said
mass. All the monks would then gather again for the service of
Lauds at dawn. This was followed by six more communal prayer
services throughout the day—about seven hours of praying together in total—the last of which is called Compline, from Old
French meaning "to complete," and was meant to send a monk
to bed for the night. Depending on the season of the year, they
usually went to sleep soon after 7:00 p.m.

Very little had changed since the Middle Ages in the life of
a Cistercian monk. Still, these aspects of a monk's life remain
largely the same. A current monk at Gethsemani recently reflected on the daily schedule:

The day of a Trappist is rather monotonous, but it's full of activities. It's monotonous in the sense that one day pretty much looks like another day. We get up at 3:00 in the morning and the first prayer is at 3:15. And then it's still dark, you know, and it's a nice, quiet time for reading until about 5:45 when we have Lauds, which is, you know, like a 25 minute prayer, choral prayer. Mass follows that and work begins at 8:00 in the morning. We work for four hours through, until 12:00. Then 12:15 is midday prayer, then lunch after that. We have the main meal in the middle of the day, and there's a break until None, which is at 2:15, and then work in the afternoon . . . or time to read, to do extra things. Vespers is 5:30 in the evening, supper after that, and then Compline at 7:30, and we go to bed at 8 o'clock. We still get seven hours of sleep.[3]

The outside world was rarely felt. Newspapers were not allowed, nor radios, but news of world events still reached the ears of monks like Merton who were practicing a medieval form of sign language to avoid as much audible conversation as possible. "Pass the salt" and "Pardon me," for instance, were gestured between the monks, rather than spoken. But there was no way to sign certain other things or feelings.

COMPELLED TO WRITE

Having entered the monastery intending to stop writing altogether, to be a man of prayer instead, he was asked by his abbot to reconsider. Merton thought that becoming a monk would mean no more novels (reading them *or* writing them), no more poems, no more writing about himself, others, or events in the world—which he was leaving behind. But his abbot told him that a life of self-denial could still involve writing, if one was meant to pray and write, both. Again, years later, when teaching the Desert Fathers to the novices, Merton would find this tension in their writings. Every monk of every era who leaves the world must face it. Merton quotes Philoxenos of Mabbug, saying: "Man is born from one world into another when he passes from the rule of the world to the rule of Christ. . . . When a man is in the world he is subject to a rule that demands that he do all those things of the world; when he is gone out after Jesus it is demanded of him that he fulfill the spiritual law, according to the order of the place into which he is come."[4] This new "spiritual law" apparently was evolving, subject to spiritual direction and the will of his abbot. So, the obedient wrote once again—in service of the church, and as part of an ascetic life.

First came poems. Poems can be very much like prayers, and they were for Merton. He had studied Gerard Manley Hopkins (convert to Catholicism, who became a priest, and whose poetry astounded the world after his death), and wrote a thesis on William Blake at Columbia, another mystical poet. As a novice, who was now named "Brother Louis," Merton saw his first published book in poems. After showing a folder of them to his old professor Mark Van Doren, Van Doren shared them with a young publisher named James Laughlin, who had recently started a firm called New Directions with money given to him by his father for graduating Harvard. The resulting volume, *Thirty*

Poems, included some autobiographical reflections by Merton on his experiences in Harlem at Friendship House, as well as a powerful poem on the tragic death of his younger brother, John Paul. Some of the poems are strident, theologically and didactically. These qualities would steadily diminish in the years to come.

Next came the autobiography.

The religious certainty that fills the pages of *The Seven Storey Mountain* can be surprising to readers who come to Merton first in his later work—and almost all his books are "later work" compared to the earliest poems and *The Seven Storey Mountain.*

In the autobiography, Merton adopted a perspective that wasn't original to him but that he made most compelling—suggesting that the world's center was in out-of-the-way places like a Trappist monastery in rural Kentucky, because prayer is what holds everything together. This message resonated deeply with readers who were living in the wake of the catastrophic events of the Second World War: the horrors of the Holocaust, the carpet bombing of German cities, the dropping of atomic bombs. The world was terrified in the summer of 1945, midway through the early period of Merton's life as a novice, when the United States dropped the first atomic bombs on Hiroshima and Nagasaki in Japan, killing hundreds of thousands of civilians instantly. We can imagine what he thought of this, given the powerful anti-war essays he would later produce, but he was in no place to write or publish on such subjects, not for many years to come.

Could there truly be a place in the world that still has the power to hold all things together and for good? Merton said that he had found it.

It wasn't a message designed to appeal to people who had experienced traumatic events. Today, a writer will often craft a message that's timely, tapping into current events or the predominant mood, with a desire to create a meaningful work of art that strikes a chord with readers. That's not what Merton did. He had written in his journal in 1941 while on retreat at Gethsemani eight months before coming back as a novice: "This is the center of America. I had wondered what was holding the country together, what has been keeping the universe from cracking in pieces and falling apart. It is places like this monastery."[5] But the power of this notion was received as one tremendous hope when it was published seven years later.

"This is the center of America," he wrote at the beginning of *The Seven Storey Mountain* with a flurry of intensity, sentences pouring out of him.

This confident sense of mission and conversion also helped determine the opinions he would put forward in his bestselling book and its very setting. The seven stories of the title are an allusion to Dante's epic poem about Purgatory: the divinely created kingdom where every human soul must be cleansed if it wants to ascend to heaven. Dante's *Purgatory* has seven terraces, each representing one of the seven mortal sins that captivate and trap human beings. These are, in ascending order: pride, envy, wrath, sloth, avarice, gluttony, and lust.

So this is serious business—life.

Much later, Merton would express embarrassment over his autobiography, because of that certainty—as if he had all the answers then. He came to see, as we often do as we grow older, that we clearly don't. We often don't even know all the right questions, at those times when we think we have all the answers.

He was also uncomfortable with *The Seven Storey Mountain* later, because it is part of what made him famous. Like any writer, I suspect that he had wanted to be respected—in the ways that an intellectual is respected, with people longing to hear what he has to say—but not famous in the way of a celebrity. Celebrity status made him uncomfortable as an author and then panic-stricken as a monk.

Still midway through his preparations for the priesthood, and before he was ready and allowed to take his final vows as a monk of Gethsemani, Br. Louis received notices from his agent and publisher that his autobiography would be published. He'd written the manuscript with excitement and anticipation but had been waiting to hear if it would ever see the light of day. Such a book by a monk hadn't been written in 1,500 years. One can only imagine how his fellow monks felt about it when they were told.

The Seven Storey Mountain outsold every other nonfiction book published in 1948. In 1949, the sales continued, astonishing everyone involved with the book. In the first six months of publication, *Time* magazine alone published three articles about its author and the book's astonishing success. The first of these appeared six weeks after publication and grasped the truth of the situation: spiritual pilgrims were drawn to the story of a fellow seeker who wasn't taking the easy approach to answering vital questions:

Last week a remarkable book called The Seven Storey Mountain *(Harcourt Brace; $3), the autobiography of a young poet who became a Trappist monk (TIME, Oct. 11), was a bestseller in its fifth printing. Thomas Merton's book was not designed to entertain; it does not offer readers escape—or tips on how to be popular or successful. In fact, the popular and successful reader may be made most uncomfortable by* The Seven Storey Mountain.[6]

This was a time when the bestselling nonfiction book in the world had been, for a decade, Dale Carnegie's *How to Win Friends and Influence People.*

Fame came quickly to Merton as readers wanted to know more about him and what made him "tick." He didn't want celebrity status, which is the complete opposite of being a monk. In correspondence with his publisher, Robert Giroux, concluding a letter that confirmed the date of his upcoming ordination, he asked his old friend: "[P]ray for me to become the simplest of all priests!"[7] But, prayers or not, that wouldn't happen.

Merton's religious certainty and enthusiasm pressed into every corner of his religious life and his written work, which continued to expand. For example, long hours spent every day in a hot or cold church singing the psalms in Latin beside other sweating or freezing monks became moments, for Fr. Louis, of near rapture. In a book on the Psalms, *Bread in the Wilderness,* published in 1953, he rhapsodizes in a way that would wear off a decade later: "There is no purer praise of God than we find in the Psalms. If we make that purity our own, we lay ourselves open as targets, which fire from heaven can strike and consume: and this is all our desire, and God's desire for us."[8]

His convictions were of the sort that one often finds in earnest converts, where the tenets and experiences of faith feel more momentous than they do to those who grew up among them. The opening line of one of his early poems, "Trappists, Working," reflects these early monastic days and working in the fields with the other monks: "Now all our saws sing holy sonnets in this world of timber." (!)

He felt like a man who was grateful to have escaped the world's clutches. He was ascending those terraces of Purgatory with intentionality and verve. It was the religious scholar and satirist Erasmus who remarked five hundred years earlier that monks and friars had tried to lure him into the monastery by saying, Remember the traveler in the woods who sat upon a tree only to realize, when it was too late, that the tree was really a snake, and that the world devours those who try to make a home in it. Erasmus used this anecdote to say that he hadn't been fooled into blaming the world. But, in his early books, Merton did just that.

Another early poem on the Passion of Christ is telling—full of words such as *jaws, flesh, blood, raging, tears, lecher, wastes, death, bones, skull, angry, ruins, burning, agony, cut,* and *gall.*[9] It was published in late 1946, just after the world had fallen apart again in Europe. Certainties of culture and civilization had vanished. There were those in the church like Merton, pointing to the truth of Christ as the only truth that was left. (Meanwhile, others, with good reason, were saying, "How could God be left if this has happened to the world?") But Merton would have trouble recognizing lines such as these as his two decades later.

One thing wouldn't change from the early writings to the later ones: he would always speak from a place and platform that was clearly defined, but in an idiom that had a way of communicating almost universally to the spiritual needs and desires of people everywhere.

TRYING TO BE QUIET

For a quiet monk who wanted nothing to do with fame, he sure published a lot. Every honest writer will tell you that there is always some ego involved in publishing a book. There almost has to be. One could think one's thoughts without seeking their publication. To publish is to want to be heard, to desire an audience. The still-young Fr. Louis showed himself to very much want to be heard.

Even the death of his abbot was not something he would experience in silence or express simply with his brother monks. Dom Frederic Dunne died while traveling to Georgia, where a daughter monastery was being formed twenty miles from Atlanta. His death took place in early August 1948, just two months before the publication of *The Seven Storey Mountain*. Merton wrote about it in a journal he was keeping then, which would be published less than four and a half years later as *The Sign of Jonas*. It, too, would be a bestseller.

The appeal of *The Sign of Jonas* was because it told the backstory of what Merton was doing and thinking while *The Seven Storey Mountain* was written, published, and becoming a bestseller. So, first, a cloistered monk wrote an autobiography, and then he published a private journal! It was unheard of for one to talk and write so much.

In the opening to part 2, "Death of an Abbot," Merton says this, almost as if he had no choice:

> When a man becomes "an author" in the world outside, he adapts himself comfortably to the situation by imitating the other authors he meets at parties. An author in a Trappist monastery is like a duck in a chicken coop. And he would give anything in the world to be a chicken instead of a duck.

I don't exactly believe him. Except for the reference to authors at parties (he surely meant the cocktail variety, common in New York City literary circles), Merton was doing everything else at this time that an eager author does, and with gusto: corresponding with publishers, his agent, media, readers. He was involved in every aspect of how he was published, including cover designs and interior presentations. He was recommending people to whom to send review copies who might influence the market for each book. He was absorbed in a writer's work. So by his actions, he was clearly a duck who knew that he lived in a chicken coop. So why did he give an otherwise impression? I think it's because he still had the ideal vision in his mind of what a monk was supposed to be. For years, he kept referring to that ideal.

I again find him disingenuous (consciously? unconsciously?) when he blames his dead abbot for ordering him to write. The now-famous monk is lamenting his fame—in print, in another soon-to-be bestseller that had been eagerly packaged by author and publisher to appeal to the audience of the autobiography:

> *It was he who firmly and kindly encouraged me and indeed ordered me. . . . I really think Dom Frederic was more interested in* The Seven Storey Mountain *than I was.*[10]

His abbot had encouraged him. The censors of his religious order had approved his work, despite frequent misgivings. But Merton was the engine behind all his writing. I think Merton was in a fight with Fr. Louis.

On the very first page of the prologue of *The Sign of Jonas,* he was dishonest, at least with himself. But in this instance, I will show you how his great gift benefited all of us whose religious and spiritual practice have been enhanced by monastic wisdom. His opening sentence—

> *This book . . . was not written with any thought that it might be read by persons unfamiliar with the monastic life.*[11]

—cannot possibly be true. It was how Merton revealed the mysteries of monastic life to people outside the monastery, who knew nothing of the monastery before reading his books, that was his greatest gift as a writer and teacher of Christian spirituality.

He was, all at the same time, deeply authentic, personally idealistic, and disingenuous. I think he shows that it is possible to combine all of those at once. He surely knew that his fellow monks did not want to read his journaling about being a monk. He wasn't writing for them. He was writing for those in "the world" that he'd left behind. He was writing for all people who have to face the seven terraces of the Purgatory mountain of the world, hoping to transcend it, to be welcomed into the earthly paradise. Yet, his instincts as a writer of the spiritual life were more adept than anyone else's. He knew very well what would draw the non-monastic spiritual-seeking pilgrim in books. He did all of that so well, in fact, that we still find him and his books all these years later!

MORE AND MORE WRITING

With the success that these bestselling books and features in *Time* magazine brought him came more attention upon not just Merton but the quiet Abbey of Gethsemani. Also, young men began to flock there to become novices in much greater numbers, many of them influenced by having read Merton. The increase in population led to the necessity for more accommodations. Building projects commenced, and the existing community felt the squeeze.

So while Merton was fighting with the noise inside himself, he was also becoming frustrated by the noise in and around the monastery.

"It is in deep solitude that I find the gentleness with which I can truly love my brothers," he wrote in his journal in January 1950.[12] This doesn't sound like what a monk learns in the Rule of St. Benedict about learning the virtues of living in community. It sounds more akin to, *I find it easiest to love others when I'm not forced to be with them all the time, and not reminded of what I don't like about them.* He was like most of us in that simply loving our neighbor could be the most difficult thing to do in real daily life.

This was also a time when a variety of health problems began to pop up and plague him. There would be lung ailments, back pain, and stomach pain, soon diagnosed as colitis. He had false teeth before he turned fifty. Between an increasingly busy monastic life and writing and collecting royalties from books he published, he sometimes pondered what was the purpose of it all.[13]

On January 13, 1950, he signed a contract with the publisher of *The Seven Storey Mountain* to write four more books. He viewed that contract as a turning point regarding his vocation: now he knew what it was. He had been self-conscious about his "work" as a Trappist, since he was most often at his typewriter during the work hours of each day, when most of his able-bodied brothers were lifting hay bales, rebuilding stone walls, milking cows, or otherwise sweating to work in the ways St. Benedict praised in his Rule. The physical exhaustion of traditional monastic work was only infrequently experienced by Fr. Louis. His work resembled what he'd been doing before he came to the abbey.

He'd been thinking and praying about his monastic life, feeling dissatisfaction in his progress toward its ideals of continual prayer and unitive experience of God, but now, resolved to write, and quite a bit at that, he was making a decision that would impact everything else. No longer would he worry about being quieter. This contract was a verification of sorts that said he was doing what God had designed him to do.

Signing that four-book contract meant he could stop thinking about whether his situation was good or bad. He would delve in, do his best at the work he was given, and stop worrying so much over whether his monastic vocation was of the right kind. Merton said to himself: "That means the final renouncement forever of any dream of a Charterhouse or a hermitage. . . . [M]y work is my hermitage."[14]

TEACHING AND OPEN QUESTIONS

His cumulative royalties, by 1954, had paid his monastery more than $1 million. But it probably won't surprise you to hear that he was not resolved in himself, once and for all, that his work would be his hermitage. The stirrings of desire for quiet and solitude remained very much in and with him.

In 1955, after pleading for a more contemplative life, and suggesting that he might need to leave for a different religious order where solitude was easier to obtain, his abbot responded with compassion and smart business acumen: he promoted him. In October of that year, Fr. Louis was asked by Abbot Dom James to be the abbey's novice master, leaving Merton responsible for teaching theology and the history of spirituality to the novices. He began to do this with gusto and pride. In fact, he soon exhausted himself doing it. One very positive result for the rest of us is the hundreds of hours we have of recordings of his lectures to the young men studying to become Trappist monks.

There are many firsthand accounts describing what he was like as a novice master. There are even monks still living at Gethsemani today who knew Fr. Louis in that capacity. He was well loved. "His honest concern for the individual and his sheer joy made life at Gethsemani, at least initially, one of growth and happiness," wrote one man, who in fact ended up leaving the monastery at age twenty-one, four years after arriving as a teenager. He goes on to explain:

> The most wonderful part of my experience at Gethsemani was having Fr. Louis as a spiritual advisor. Each of the novices met with him individually quite frequently and he gave us all the time we needed to let out our frustrations and desires and to seek help with meditation and monastic tensions. In my case I found that we laughed a lot and the conversations strayed to many non-spiritual areas. We often spoke of New York City, me being a Brooklynite and he a sometime resident. (Some of the novices signed me that they used to sit around near Louie's office just to hear the laughter when we were having our time together.)

Then he adds, picturesquely:

> Fr. Louis had a quite distinctive walk. He could often be seen with three or four books under his arm, heading for a quiet spot in the woods. He sort of bounced when he walked and the novices had many good laughs imitating his hop. (He was affectionately known as Uncle Louie to some of the monks in later years.) When you were sitting outside his office and the door was open you could hear how fast he was reading a new book from France by how quickly he cut through the folios when the pages had not been cut at the factory. Zip, zip, zip!

*Phenomenal speed. Fr. Louis' personality was outgoing, warm
and full of humor. When you were speaking with him you felt
as if you were the most important person in his life and that
his honesty and good will sprang from the depths of his soul.*[15]

So the desire for greater silence to pursue a contemplative vocation did not mean that he was not fun to be around. Merton was
gregarious and a friend to many.

Also, by 1955, after several books and nearly a decade and a
half in the monastery, Fr. Louis began to talk of questions that
"have no answers." He said, "We must be silent in the presence
of signs whose meaning is closed to us." But it was somewhat
fleeting—this reverent attitude toward mystery—still. One sees
him struggling with himself in these matters in a beautiful book
from his mid-career titled *No Man Is an Island.* Then he returns,
only a paragraph later, to that familiar tone of certainty, with
statements such as:

*If I am to know the will of God, I must have the right attitude
toward life. I must first of all know what life is, and to know
the purpose of my existence.*[16]

How did this fit with his growing understanding that questions often don't have answers? He even recognized that his
writing—as a priest and monk expected to follow official teachings of the church at every turn—was popular with ordinary
people because of his willingness to reveal doubts. He said, "It
seems to me that one of the reasons why my writing appeals to
many people is precisely that I am not sure of myself and do

not claim to have all the answers."[17] What is (will always be) a weakness to some ideologically driven Christians is what endears him to millions of others. Admitting to not having all the answers means being ready to listen. This would grow in him.

He gradually came to see that being a true contemplative meant listening more than it meant teaching and talking. This was the beginning of his coming to understand a more mature, full sense of freedom in God, which would inform and transform all his relationships.[18]

The audience for his writing also grew. *No Man Is an Island* quickly went from hardcover into a mass market paperback edition selling for thirty-five cents. By then, another of his early popular books, *Seeds of Contemplation,* was already in its fifth printing as a mass market paperback—these are the books that used to sell in magazine and cigar shops and at grocery store checkout lines—priced at twenty-five cents.[19] That's about $2.30 in today's money.

He began producing books of short bursts of inspiration. Many of his best books, in fact—such as *Seeds of Contemplation, No Man Is an Island, Thoughts in Solitude,* and later, *The Way of Chuang Tzu* (Merton's favorite of his own work) and *Conjectures of a Guilty Bystander,* were epigrammatic and aphoristic in style. At the time—this was the 1950s—this struck many readers as odd. Today, it is much more common and is probably another reason why his writing remains popular.

He missed some things. For example, in talking about spiritual matters, he ignored what we know today as clinical depression—which is not surmountable regardless of Christian cheer. And he unfortunately calls "despair" "the absolute extreme of self-love." This is the sort of lack of understanding of mental illness, and emotional distress, that has stigmatized therapy, suicide, and clinical depression for centuries. In this way, some of Merton's writing can seem old-fashioned and out of date, even in one of his most enduring and important books, *New Seeds of Contemplation:*

> *Despair is the ultimate development of a pride so great and so stiff-necked that it selects the absolute misery of damnation rather than accept happiness from the hands of God.*[20]

But to be fair, very few people understood these matters until sometime after Merton's death in 1968. Outside the religious realm—which could and can be terribly unfair by proscribing "cheerfulness" and "hope" when therapy is what's called for—words like *melancholy* and *hypochondria* were used not long ago to describe what we now know as forms of serious depression.

Even some of Merton's comments about himself, written during his early years as a monk, published in the autobiography and journals, would be treated differently today from how they were then. For example, he wrote this, which will likely sound familiar to you by now, since we understand how he framed leaving "the world" behind: "By the grace of God it was easy for me to forget the world as soon as I left it."[21] But a young man saying this in the monastery today would likely be sent to see a therapist.

4

In a Furnace of Ambivalence

That first decade and a half in the monastery gave Merton something in common with the original hermit-monk, St. Anthony, who lived at the end of Roman antiquity in the Egyptian desert. Like Merton, St. Anthony lived on the outskirts of Christendom. Both men left urban cityscapes and culture for the wiles of monastic wildernesses. Anthony left the cities of the Roman Empire for the unknown, uncivilized desert—to test his faith there. Merton wanted nothing more than a life of simple obedience and silence when he entered a monastery in rural Kentucky, far from New York City where he'd once felt so comfortable. Like Anthony, Merton intended to leave cities and civilization behind.

Then look at what happened. His writing success, combined with the way that the Second World War disillusioned an entire generation, led to a flood of novices walking through those iron gates that had closed Merton inside his freedom. He no longer felt so free. From 1941 to 1956, he must have moved through a lifetime of feelings and experiences. Out of all this comes one of his most essential teachings.

TRUE SELF, FALSE SELF

The ways in which he was dishonest with himself made his pursuit of personal truth all the more important. Attempting to honestly discern who he was, and distinguish this from who he might be pretending to be, was an act of deepest faith and trust. This is something that every person, regardless of religious tradition, has to undergo and only sometimes does it feel that one is succeeding.

How do we "hear" God's intentions? One way, Merton's Cistercian tradition taught him, was to listen for God in what you feel is inauthentic about yourself. Learn to see and hear and feel what is the real you responding to God in your life, and what is false.

A monastery assists in this. Every young monk has an abbot and a novice master. Each monk has a spiritual director and confessor. The stereotype we have is of a monk who lives alone. "Alone for God" is above the gate as one enters the Abbey of Gethsemani even today, as it did when Tom Merton first arrived. A monk is one who is willing to be alone. The word itself has its root in the ancient Greek *monachos,* meaning "solitary." But this is only part of a monastic life. There are also tools for not being alone. Everyone needs friends and mentors on the spiritual path.

The word from which monk is derived, *monachos,* also means "only" and "unique." Merton's joy came in discovering in the

Christian mystical tradition a rich understanding for how to un-
cover his true self in the midst of all the many ways, consciously
and unconsciously, that we encourage in our lives a false self.
Sometimes he would teach directly on this matter, translating the
wisdom from medieval sources such as St. Bernard of Clairvaux,
the spiritual father of the Cistercian approach in monasticism,
and at other times Merton's approach and tone struck a chord
that simply celebrated the true self—in himself and others.

For example, in a book of poems finished near the end of his
life, just before he left for Asia, called *Cables to the Ace,* he begins
with lines that sound like they're almost straight out of the poems of the great American poet Walt Whitman. "I am . . . ," he
says, "I am," over and over. It is not quite Whitman's famous
opening line, "I celebrate myself," but it is Merton's satisfaction
with singularity and ultimate rest in his true self. How did he get
there?

Gerard Manley Hopkins, whom Merton also admired, had this
self-confidence, too, and had admired it in Whitman. "I always
knew in my heart Walt Whitman's mind to be more like my own
than any other man's living," Hopkins once wrote, which is kind
of shocking from a Jesuit religious poet who is often dogmat-
ically conservative in his ideas.[1] What united them all was a
thorough understanding of the true self.

The way that Merton came to understand this is most beautiful and important for every spiritual seeker. This is probably the
most essential of all his spiritual teachings. In his own words,
here is its essence in three short sentences:

First, "Every one of us is shadowed by an illusory person: a
false self."[2] Consider all that we do, often daily, even more often

than that, not to engage with who we are truly meant to be. Simply on a physical level—we use entertainments, food, sex, overwork, stimulants, and other things to evade our true selves.

Second, "This is the man I want myself to be but who cannot exist, because God does not know anything about him." (You'll have to forgive those masculine pronouns in his writing; I hope you do forgive them.) While doing those things, we think we're happy, but we are not. Most importantly, God doesn't know the person who is evading and escaping. God knows who we truly are.

Third—this is contrary to what every monk and would-be monk wants for their lives:

"And to be unknown of God is altogether too much privacy." The false self leads us into a *monachos* that is alone without being unique—without discovering how each one of us is, in some vital and real ways, singular ("only") before God.

He found this teaching weaving throughout the Christian mystics as he studied and taught them to the young men seeking to become monks. For example, the early sixth-century figure known as Pseudo-Denys the Areopagite says it this way:

We would be like sculptors who set out to carve a statue. They remove every obstacle to the pure view of the hidden image and simply by this act of clearing aside they reveal the beauty that is hidden.[3]

Michelangelo would echo this precisely when sculpting from stone during the Renaissance.

AN IDEAL MONASTERY

We saw in the last chapter how, in those first fifteen years in the monastery, Fr. Louis sometimes felt uncertain about *where* to live his vocation. Should he transfer to the Carthusians, a more contemplative, quiet religious order? Would he do better as a monk in a quieter monastery somewhere else? Did he need a hermitage to truly live apart?

In *The Sign of Jonas,* a journal he began writing five years in, he wrote about the ideal monastery being a place of reading, meditation, contemplative prayer, and prayer that continues during manual work. Then, he said, "But now, let us suppose that within four or five years, several hundred men decide that they want lives [like this]. And suppose they all decide to enter the same monastery."[4] That's of course exactly what happened.

He goes on for another page to say that 270 men were "packed into a building that was built for seventy." So new buildings have to be built, and construction equipment is everywhere. Priests and novice directors are needed to care for and form these young men who have arrived seeking to become monks, and there is extra work for everyone. There is no longer much silence. No one could have foreseen this, but it gives him pause.

It was "a moment of crisis and transition," as Merton described, while standing in the midst of it. As a result, he felt he was stuck in "a furnace of ambivalence."[5] This was, in some respects, only the next in the series of crises for a man who had come to see his life through such lenses.

There could be—there surely are—deeper reasons still. It could be that the autobiography, the published private journals,

all the writing, with all the success and power that it communicated to the still-young Merton, was enough to cause him to
lose the fervor for simple obedience. How ironic that would be,
if true, since the young monk only wrote that first famous book
because his abbot encouraged him to do so. Merton's first publisher, James Laughlin, believed this. He wrote after his friend's
death:

> When he first came to the monastery in 1941, he had all the
> proper attitudes of a postulant, then those of a novice, then
> those of a young priest. He was humble, he was obedient,
> he fully believed that whatever the abbot said was what he
> should do. But later, as he matured, had his success, and real-
> ized his power as a writer, his perception of his role began to
> change. . . . [H]e saw what he could do with his writing, and
> this gave him more confidence to be himself.[6]

Laughlin goes on to say that the mature writer and man remained
obedient, ultimately, to his vocation and to his religious superiors, but it came to be more on his terms.

How could the monk who was so often upset about his own
lack of quiet and solitude also become the most loquacious of
communicators? He enjoyed correspondence with hundreds of
people, including the most renowned literary and religious people of his day—from Russian poet Boris Pasternak to folk singer
Joan Baez to Pope John XXIII. Merton thought he'd left the world
behind, quite literally, before his abbot instructed him to sit at a
typewriter in an office, during work hours, and tell his life story.
Look what happened.

There's a letter, for instance, that he wrote to one of his publishers in February 1948, several months before *The Seven Storey Mountain* would be published and make him famous, and in it he begins with a confession: "The devil is trying to mess up all that I do by getting me to do too much and involve me in such a network of projects that I will be neither able to work or pray." Then he goes on to detail his writing projects one by one. Fr. Abbot is annoyed that one of the monk's books of poems is out of stock. The monk needs a Spanish text of St. John of the Cross to work more on a project that's been previously discussed. The monk needs to write more poems. Meanwhile, another book—which he calls his "book of *pensées*"—is coming along nicely. (This would become *Seeds of Contemplation.*) And the autobiography (*Seven Storey*) is much too long, needs trimming.[7] No wonder he had trouble balancing things and finding time to pray!

Soon, Merton was beginning to back out of community life, seeking to explore a hermit's vocation, which was then mostly unknown among the Trappists. For years, he asked his abbot for more access to time alone before being granted what he desired. He knew that in many respects he'd created his own problem; the success of his writings had brought many people to the monastery looking for what this "Thomas Merton" had discovered. He wanted to live apart from community life. For at least a decade before his death, in 1968, Fr. Louis was instructing young monks as their novice master, guiding them into a monastic life—that he was himself, in some ways, seeking to escape.

The impulse is common among creatives. For example, the famous French writer Romain Rolland, after being awarded a

Nobel Prize in Literature and protesting the First World War so vigorously that he became an outcast in French society, left for rural Switzerland. He said he was exchanging the "perpetual anxiety" of Paris for a life of silence.[8]

The mistake that many people make is to say: "Merton . . . was a famous writer who, late in life, had wearied of his fame and who, after a lifetime of giving his words to others, needed to place himself before the Unsayable."[9] I don't think that's it. He was more like the artist who hurts himself and while hurting himself creates great art. Think of Van Gogh cutting off his ear. Think of Kurt Cobain dying by suicide. Think of Dylan Thomas and Jack Kerouac drinking themselves to death, or Sylvia Plath sticking her head in the oven. From his difficult childhood onward, Merton had used his art to seek understanding of himself, knowing full well his flaws, offering those flaws onto the pages of what he created. That didn't change late in his life. Perhaps, rather, he came to see the flaws themselves as a natural part of a flawed self, seeking salvation. The flaws wouldn't necessarily go away. He began to see to the other side of them.

He saw giving up his public life as a step of finality that he was willing to take. For instance, after an afternoon meditating in the woods in the spring before he died, he wrote in his private journal: "I really enjoyed being in the wild, silent spot. . . . And really I am ready to let the writing go to the dogs if necessary, and to prefer this: which is what I really want and what I am here for." But then of course a guest from Boston arrives, as planned, that evening. We who love Merton and learn from him must accept how he often contradicts himself. This realization can be frustrating at times, and helpful in others. He sometimes comes across almost fickle. Truth is, he was constantly "working out" his understanding on paper; he left it for us to see, and we go looking for it. (My fickleness and other weaknesses are much more private.) Thus, we have him writing about being "in the wild, silent spot" and saying that this is who he truly is, all while guests are due to arrive, with whom he'll chat the night away, discussing things of the world. Similarly, he struggled for years with thoughts of leaving, or finding a situation that was better. We have to reconcile this with what he writes near the end of chapter 35 of that classic, *New Seeds of Contemplation:*

> *Fickleness and indecision are signs of self-love.*
>
> *If you can never make up your mind what God wills for you, but are always veering from one opinion to another, from one practice to another, from one method to another, it may be an indication that you are trying to get around God's will and do your own with a quiet conscience.*
>
> *As soon as God gets you in one monastery you want to be in another.*[10]

He's writing at times to himself.

An analogy may be helpful: My wife and I like to take long bike rides. The purpose of a good bike ride is, for her, mostly about the exercise. She's an athlete and I'm not. The exercise of a ride is, for me, only one part. So, when we plan a ride, I prefer that we also be headed somewhere: a park, a tavern, downtown, a friend's house. Simply hauling down a bike path, turning around, and coming back, doesn't really interest me. For me, the journey (or the ride) is not enough by itself, whereas it is enough for my wife as good exercise. I want to feel, also, as if I'm going somewhere. I think that Merton wished he could feel about the spiritual life the way my wife feels about bike rides—with a sort of purity of intention—but he couldn't really do that. For whatever reason, he found that that wasn't in him. In the end, he wanted to be going somewhere.

Most importantly, we should all be so self-aware, as Merton was, and so willing to reconsider who we are as we are on a journey of lifelong conversion.

GROWING INTO A VOCATION

He also shows us—in his life and spirituality—what it means to live into our ideals. He had come to the monastery with feelings of certitude as to what the monastery was and who he would be in it. But he soon realized that religious and spiritual lives are not that neat and tidy. A monastic vocation is complicated in the ways that a vocation to be married is complicated. Compromises must be made. Expectations may be met, exceeded, and sometimes lowered. There are ups and downs. There are disappointments. We bring ourselves to our religious and spiritual ideals, and we cause ourselves to make changes to our expectations. Merton shows that this is normal; it is not capitulation. It is part of growing and becoming who we are meant to be.

So, the monk who had wanted so badly to be quiet and anonymous was soon able to see, on the contrary: "But talking also helps my prayer."[11]

He was an exemplary monk, according to his contemporaries in the cloister. Even in those years immediately after the autobiography became a bestseller and he had become strangely and suddenly famous, Fr. Louis remained a fairly simple, good monk. When he was asked to join in the manual work of the monastery, he threw his body into it. When he was expected to be gracious in small things around the monastery, he was. When another monk needed a kind word, he could expect Fr. Louis to provide one. He was known by his brothers as warm and of good spirit.[12]

The furnace of ambivalence feelings came to him in these years after the autobiography made him famous and turned his monastery into a bustling place, but he kept his feelings largely to himself.

HIS GIFT TO MONKS IN THE WORLD

We who hope to accomplish in our lives what Merton wrote about seeking and accomplishing in his have to be circumspect because we are without most of the measures and disciplines to guide us in the way that monks—even somewhat rebellious ones like Merton—are. There are many ways today to live like monks do. Books are written on the subject, and small intentional-living communities are often formed of those on this path. Some of today's "neo-monasticism" (that's what it often is called) is lived online or digitally, or by people following liturgical prayer patterns that relate to what monks do in actual living communities. These are ways of being monastic, but the circumspection I'm suggesting is for when this monk-like living is without adherence to vows of obedience, stability, and poverty. Those vows relate to other people living and challenging you in real time and place; without them, it can be difficult to return after falling away. The word *conversion* means "return."

Fr. Louis was bound to his monastery, his fellow monks, and his abbot as his father. He was constantly writing in his journal, talking with his abbot, and writing letters to other friends, religious and nonreligious, revealing his faults and describing how he was intending to do better.

In *The Sign of Jonas,* he wrote, "The whole meaning of [a monk's] vocation is summed up in [his] vows. . . . They deliver him from the uncertainties and cares and illusions that beset the man of the world."[13] Even when he became famous, and even when he broke his vows, he would return to them and find the meaning of his vocation, and his very life, in them.

"I am trying to be a monk," he wrote to one priest-friend, adding that he knew how his writing and fame were getting in the way of his desire for holiness, admitting that it would be ideal if "the name of Thomas Merton can be forgotten."[14] They helped and challenged him. They also helped him to figure out that true self as distinct from the false one. Without such vows, and friends keeping him to his vows, he might have easily left Gethsemani for a quieter place.

As another monk recently described the vow of stability: "This relationship with a single monastery is a distinctive Benedictine [Trappists are Benedictine] characteristic. . . . A Benedictine monk or nun can visit another monastery where customs are familiar. He or she can even live there for a time, but it will never become home. Home is where one has made the vow of stability."[15]

Merton fell away often, and not only in his mind and spirit as he yearned to go somewhere else. There was also a time when he had a brief torrent of an affair with a student nurse we know as "M." She was a nurse in Louisville. This is a story told in full in the next chapter. He fell away in both big and small ways. His private journals are full of these accounts. (Thank God, no one will ever read mine or yours.)

This takes us to the heart of why Merton compels our attention. He found what mysticism promises. The very passions that guided his life into mistakes also steered him to what the mystic in every person so deeply desires. As James Finley, who was once a novice under Merton at Gethsemani, has said, "There is no contemplation without desire."[16]

Even more important, and more practically, true conversion is impossible without some real renunciation. In addition to obedience, stability, and poverty, a monk practices solitude, fasting, penance, and renouncing pride and ambition. As usual, Merton says it best: "[These] negative elements . . . are all intended to clear the way so that prayer, meditation and contemplation may fill the space created by the abandonment of other concerns."[17]

We also realize today what some who were carefully reading Merton a generation or two ago may have missed. It was once assumed that a contemplative—rather than "active"— life was best safeguarded and made possible by things like monastery gates, grilles of convents, the choir in Trappist life, and veils on nuns. Then we came to realize and acknowledge that the men and women who live in these ways can be just as noncontemplative as are those who are immersed in a variety of activities. Shutting up and away does not a contemplative make.

Carlo Carretto, an Italian ascetic of the last century, a vowed religious brother who lived for a decade alone as a hermit in the desert of the Sahara, wrote about this with regard to his own mother. Carretto reflected that he, who'd studied contemplative spirituality and had spent thousands of hours in meditation, was not as contemplative a person as his own mother who had done none of these things, but who had raised several children. What Carretto said was that a contemplative life is made by learning selflessness, not by living in quiet or sitting for long periods of time. A breviary also won't instill it in you. Perhaps God does it as a divine gift. But I think that Merton and Carretto also demonstrate that it is a discipline, and that the discipline is to practice losing and forgetting yourself—which is not something many of us go seeking.

5

Needing Intimacy and Love

At several points in *The Seven Storey Mountain,* Merton writes about the novelist and philosopher Aldous Huxley. Like many of his generation, Merton had tracked with Huxley, reading his novels and following his ideas. Huxley was a prominent intellectual at a time when popular culture paid attention to intellectuals. But when Merton writes about Huxley in his autobiography, he's beginning his conversion to Christianity and Catholicism, and he seems uninterested.

He had difficulty assimilating the "new Huxley" who in 1937, in *Ends and Means,* began to appreciate blessedness, religion, and mystics.* Merton read *Ends and Means* the year it was published, just when he was preparing to be baptized. He wrote enthusiastically about it for the school paper at Columbia. In the book,

---

* By any account, *Ends and Means* was a brilliant book. For example, in the first fifty pages, Huxley predicted that a full-scale Second World War was coming soon and that Britain would soon no longer be an imperial power.

Huxley had said, "The worship of one God has been abandoned in favour of the worship of such local divinities as the nation, the class and even the deified individual." And "Closely associated with the regression in charity is the decline in men's regard for truth. At no period of the world's history has organized lying been practised so shamelessly or, thanks to modern technology, so efficiently or on so vast a scale."[1] The voice and message resemble essays that Merton would later write.

But a decade later, after his conversion—to Catholicism, monasticism, Christian mysticism, to a certainty and truth he would later realize had been overzealously communicated—Merton reduced Huxley in *The Seven Storey Mountain* to a thinker to be bypassed. Why?

In the same way, Merton showed little interest in other popular figures of his day who were creating new ways of approaching spiritual problems by blending teachings of religious traditions and masters. Names like Besant, Krishnamurti, Gurdjieff, Gibran, Tagore, and a few others were a new breed of spiritual teachers without religious tradition homes. As a young monk, Merton had little use for them, too. Eventually, he would come to find truth in religious traditions other than Christianity. He would eventually enthusiastically embrace aspects of other traditions in ways that still make many of conservative Catholics uneasy. But not for a while yet.

His problem with Huxley was a problem I suspect he would have with most of us today, which is that we are generally looking for answers to our problems without using religious sources. We have become accustomed to thinking that truth doesn't live in religion. God is not as resident in our religious traditions as much as in the lives and minds of people everywhere. Appeals to the "perennial philosophy" of all teachings, or the "universal" in all spiritual people, by folks like Huxley and Gibran seemed to Merton to be a mistake.

For example, imagine a bucketful of firm round balls. Each of the balls is small enough to fit in your hand and sturdy enough to toss in the air. But each ball is a different color, made of a different material or fabric. A talented performer strolls up and picks up that bucket of balls. He grabs each ball, considers it, and then tosses it into the air. One ball follows upon another as the juggler keeps them all up in the air, tossing them around in a circle that's fascinating to watch. Those balls are the religious traditions. The juggler is the mystic like Gibran or Huxley.

To our mindset today, Merton may be old-fashioned. He was always looking for truth in religious traditions. He didn't want them blended together like a bunch of balls flying through the air. But he was a groundbreaking figure in bringing people of diverse religious backgrounds together in conversation in pursuit of understanding.

Merton's engagement in and with other religious traditions was driven by friendships, curiosity, and a sense of affirmation. Merton wrote:

> [Dialogue] does not mean syncretism, indifferentism, the vapid and careless friendliness that accepts everything by thinking of nothing. There is much that one cannot "affirm" and "accept," but first one must say "yes" where one really can.

Recent statements by some cardinals in the Catholic Church demonstrate that this is not at all a universally agreed-upon principle.[2] Merton was on the cusp of something in interreligious friendship and conversation that remains more advanced than what we probably have today.

His tenor changed in the sixties when he began to see the spiritual wisdom and mystical points of other traditions and found them similar to his own. Just as he learned how to experience opposites inside of himself, often tugging in different directions, he also learned how to appreciate that wisdom of all sorts rises up from the experience of seeming opposites. He would soon describe wisdom as "the hidden attunement of opposite tensions."[3]

Then he began to learn to distrust words he'd been using for so long. One of our most interesting contemporary writers today, Paul Kingsnorth, has recently reflected on this arc in his own life, saying, "I feel that words are savage gods and that in the end, however well you serve them, they will eat you alive."[4] Merton built a great capacity for listening to others. After his death, in fact, this is the principle thing that H. H. the Dalai Lama remembered about Merton: he was a man who could truly listen.

In other respects, though, Merton's approach to contemplation was not a product of the sixties, or of his encounter with Buddhism and Buddhist writers, which began in the fifties. His approach began early, even in his novice years at Gethsemani. From the start, he felt that his vocation was to a contemplative life. As a result, he felt it keenly when events and circumstances—both in him and around him—were working against this. Chanting the Liturgy of the Hours was the primary work of a monk, and after that, plus lessons in theology and Cistercian history, and the required manual labor, there was no time for quietly, nondiscursively *being* with God. Merton desired this way of being with God from early on. He would eventually discover that it existed in his own tradition and that his tradition had points of meeting with other Christian traditions and with mystics of the religions of the world.

This happened most of all through Zen. The opening chapter of *Zen and the Birds of Appetite,* a book of his from the sixties, goes to great lengths to tell readers that Zen is not a cultural, historical, theological thing but is a way of life that cannot be grasped in the mind. Then, with the enthusiasm of one who was already practicing Zen, referring to the scene in the book of Exodus in the Old Testament when a young Moses comes upon the famous burning bush from which he hears God's voice, Merton could write:

> [T]here eventually comes a time when like Moses we see that the thornbush of cultural and religious forms is suddenly on fire and we are summoned to approach it without shoes—and probably also without feet.[5]

Then, he compares the burning bush of Exodus to one of the Prajñāpāramitā Sutras of Mahayana Buddhism.

Merton would probably have respected a writer like Huxley if he'd encountered his books later in life. I think he also would have found friends in people like Ram Dass, Joseph Campbell (who quoted Merton's writings occasionally), and Alan Watts, the Anglican turned Zen priest. But, most of all, Merton remained comfortable with religious figures—people who were vowed members of religious traditions—such as Thich Nhat Hanh, Rabbi Zalman Schachter-Shalomi, and Daniel Berrigan, SJ. (D. T. Suzuki was more like Campbell and Watts, a willing mixer of spiritual teachings, as exemplified in his active involvement in the Theosophical Society movement. Did Merton know this? Perhaps not.)

TRUE INTIMACY

He undergoes the greatest test of his monastic vows in the spring and summer of 1966 when he meets and gets to know Margie, or "M," a student nurse in Louisville. In and out of the hospital for tests and procedures, beginning in March, he and one of the nurses begin to have frequent contact and soon fall in love, despite a great difference in their ages. Tom is fifty-one, and Margie is twenty-five. He will soon write a poem (that goes unpublished throughout his lifetime and still remains largely unavailable) that is basically a meditation on the fact that "M" was born in nearby Cincinnati at about the precise time that Merton was entering the monastery as a novice.[6]

Years earlier, in *The Seven Storey Mountain,* he had said, "[N]ever since I have entered religion have I ever had the slightest desire to go back to the world."[7] At least during the summer of "M," this was no longer true. He was briefly torn. What should he do?

There were private meetings, alone, that include lying together naked—and the monk writing ecstatically, later, about the experience. Surely, they had sex. Most Merton experts believe

this is so. But there are good reasons why Merton's most important biographer once wrote about the "M" episode in his life: "It
is a story that has been blown out of all proportion by some and
minimized by others."[8]

They certainly had an affair—an affair that probably only
stopped because a fellow monk reported to the abbot that he
overheard a lovey phone call (the monastery then used party
lines) between Merton and a woman. There's no telling what
would have happened otherwise. To make or receive such calls
shows how out of control he was then.

A couple of years later, in December 1966, when the monk
was talking at Gethsemani with Joan Baez and her husband,
those two challenged his vow of obedience. As Baez tells it:

> *Ira started pushing him: "Why don't you just go to Bangkok?"*
> *[Meaning, leave the monastery and pursue other interests, such*
> *as Eastern religion.] Merton said, "Well, that's a good idea*
> *but you don't understand this life. You take vows, and one of*
> *the vows is you do as you're told to do." But obviously some*
> *things about him were not that style at all, or he wouldn't be*
> *writing that kind of poetry, and he wouldn't be outspoken*
> *against the war in Vietnam. So we teased him about it and*
> *pushed and said, "Come on. . . . Why don't you just get up and*
> *go?" He said, "Oh, no, I can't . . ."[9]*

Merton wrote in his journal immediately after being with
Margie for a full day in the woods near his hermitage, "We do
really belong to each other," followed by, "yesterday was this
slow, gradual new stage of ripening, and the grip of this deep

warm sexual love disturbing me and flooding through me. . . .
Yet I refuse to be disturbed by it."[10] He writes to himself that he
has never experienced love like this before. No doubt, that was
absolutely true, but it troubles those who see only unfaithfulness
in his stumbling. On a simply human level, there is a kind of
triumph in Merton's discovery of the variances and depth of
love, with "M."

A few years later, he would write in a letter to a fellow Cistercian: "Love is the epiphany of God."[11] In other words, love
comes unexpectedly, and if it is love, it is always God.

But seen from the perspective of his monastic vows, one sees
the sin. This is who he was, in his humanness, but also in his
ability to keep discovering. More than any other interpretation,
I appreciate this one:

> *He came to discover that the experience of being "rapt" in
> ecstatic love could occur, not only as a private, spiritual ex-
> perience, shared by God and himself, but also in physical, in-
> timate relationship with a lover.*[12]

LOVE AND HOLINESS

A few years before he met Margie in Louisville, Fr. Louis had
studied *Hagia Sophia,* a Greek phrase that literally means "Holy
Wisdom," and which he understood to be the feminine side of
God. Like certain Christian mystics before him, Merton was in
love with *Hagia Sophia.* Perhaps his greatest poem of all is written for Her, a prose poem of the same name, "Hagia Sophia."

"She is His manifestation," Merton writes, meaning that God's principle expression in the universe is a feminine one.

He jotted some of his early notes on *Hagia Sophia* while in the hospital in Louisville on an earlier occasion. It was July 2, 1960:

> *At 5:30, as I was dreaming, in a very quiet hospital, the soft voice of the nurse awoke me gently from my dream—and it was like awakening for the first time from all the dreams of my life—as if the Blessed Virgin herself, as if Wisdom had awakened me.*

When he then published the poem three years later, it included that very reference, that he had woken up in a hospital bed on "July the second."[13] This demonstrates how Merton was prepared to see and experience love in that setting, before "M" ever entered his life. He was thirsty for it. Love was Mother. Love was Wisdom. He knew it already, but not in every respect.

As his authorized biographer once explained, "With the image of the unnamed nurse waking him in hospital Merton must have felt he had completed the full portrait of Hagia Sophia, which had been the creation of many dreams and much reading, joining all this to the actual." The biographer then suggests there may have been "an idealized Ruth Merton" (his mother who died when he was just a boy) in the dreamlike experience from that July 2. I don't know about that, but I think we can see how he was preparing himself to experience the love that he would soon experience from a very real, but still perhaps dreamlike, nurse in Louisville.

Margie never wrote a tell-all memoir. She never gave an interview to "set the record straight." This is all to her enormous
credit, even though it leaves a gap in what we know about Merton's most private relationship: his love of summer 1966.

When he was less mature, Merton often portrayed personal
holiness as the most important thing in the world. He buttressed
his exhortations to holiness with references to truth. His comments of this sort were gobbled up by religious people, as such
teachings always have been appreciated since religions began
by people who like to use them to measure themselves against
others. "Holiness is more than humanity," for instance, he said
in *Seeds of Contemplation* in 1949.[14] The experiences of maturity,
especially the unexpectedness of what happened with Margie,
taught him that love, not holiness, was the most important thing
in the world.

He wrote a beautiful essay after his relationship with "M"
ended called "Love and Need." I wish you all could read it, but
it isn't easy to find.

He says that love isn't about falling in love, in the usual way
that we use that phrase, as if we aren't responsible for what we
do in love. But then he goes on to say positively about falling in
love, "Love takes you out of yourself. You lose control." Why is
this good? It *is* good—because "the question of love is one that
cannot be evaded."

I recall once, when revelations arose a decade or so ago suggesting that Pope John Paul II might have had an emotional affair (no one really suggests that there was anything sexual about
it) with a married Polish American woman in Vermont, I said to
a journalist-priest friend of mine, "This is shocking. You should

write about this!" He replied very simply and calmly, "We all fall in love."

I see Merton's experience with Margie in this light: he fell in love, a bit out of control, surely breaking his vows, but then he returned, and that's what conversion is always about. He discovered that love is not just more important than holiness but that holiness is impossible without love. As he put it himself in that late essay:

> Love is our true destiny. We do not find the meaning of life by ourselves alone. . . . We do not discover the secret of our lives merely by study and calculation in our own isolated meditations. The meaning of our life is a secret that has to be revealed to us in love. . . . We will never be fully real until we let ourselves fall in love—either with another human person or with God.[15]

6

Moving Toward Wholeness

If this is Merton's most famous sentence from his enthusiastic autobiography—

> *So Brother Matthew locked the gate behind me and I was enclosed in the four walls of my new freedom.*

—then these are the most often quoted lines from his mid-career as a writer, spiritual seeker, and wisdom teacher:

> *In Louisville, at the corner of Fourth and Walnut, in the center of the shopping district, I was suddenly overwhelmed with the realization that I loved all those people, that they were mine and I theirs, that we could not be alien to one another even though we were strangers. It was like waking from a dream of separateness . . . the world of renunciation and supposed holiness.*[1]

He had come full circle.

Merton was no longer a triumphant Catholic, but someone who had figured out (some would call it "enlightened") how following Jesus meant discovering humanity—his own, and that of others—and the essential unity of all things in God. The large sign that marks the spot where Merton stood while he had this vision on March 18, 1958, placed there by the Commonwealth of Kentucky, reads at the top, "A Revelation."

But he was kicking himself. "To think that for sixteen or seventeen years I have been taking seriously this pure illusion that is implicit in so much of our monastic thinking," he wrote. And then, perhaps most quoted of all, he gave this description to his feelings and his new vision: "[I]f only everybody could realize this! But it cannot be explained. There is no way of telling people that they are all walking around shining like the sun."[2]

Such an experience is not uncommon for people like Merton: spiritually attuned. It is almost inevitable. Sometimes Merton devotees, frankly, make too much of Fourth and Walnut. How many spiritual adepts of his generation wrote and taught about coming to realize that they were one with everything? Many, many. It is a kind of spiritual healing for the formerly self-centered. It is a well-worn but completely necessary brick on the path.

Similarly, Merton's Fourth and Walnut experience (that's what it is often called in books about him) failed to consider the ways in which all people could *not* come together, at that time, at Fourth and Walnut. For instance, African Americans could not eat in the restaurants on the corner there. They also were not allowed to shop in the shops there, or sit in the theater and watch a movie.[3] Louisville, Kentucky, was segregated and dominated by Jim Crow when Merton had his experience of oneness. Merton's enlightenment and joy were subject to the conditions of his white comfort and privilege. To his credit, he knew this, and he would soon turn his nearly full-time attention to righting the wrongs of inequality.

In the process, however, he seems to have been feeling more and more separated from his own monastic community, and perhaps from the ideals of community itself. His next coming full circle came with his escape from community life. Long unsettled rubbing elbows with fellow monks and their quirks and noises in the monastery, Merton finally convinced his abbot to allow him to live apart. He had been homeless at fifteen. He was well rooted and at home at thirty. And he chose to be homeless, once again, at forty-five.

Was he drawn to the teachings of the Desert Fathers, early Christian mystics who lived mostly in isolation from each other, because he had lost hope in monasticism in community? Merton admitted in at least one letter to a friend around this time, "I believe God is testing the quality of my desire for solitude, in which perhaps there was an element of escape from responsibility."[4] These would be powerful words in the introduction to his 1960 collection of translated sayings of the Desert Fathers:

> In those days men had become keenly conscious of the strictly individual character of "salvation." Society . . . was regarded by them as a shipwreck from which each single individual man had to swim for his life.[5]

An odd piece of teaching, coming from a cenobitic monk who had discovered this kind of freedom when that iron gate closed behind him nineteen years earlier.

But his hermitage would not be an isolating place for him like it was for those desert monks from long ago. Entering his hermitage allowed Merton to live as a contemplative in those ways that he'd wanted to do for so long. All the evidence points to his heart softening, his ability to love others deepening, when he was finally able to spend significant time apart from the community of monks he knew and loved so well.

THE OTHER HALF OF HIS SOUL

At this time in his life, just as essential for Merton as becoming a hermit in the Western tradition was his discovery of the wisdom of the religions of the East. This was also part of his finding wholeness.

Back in 1946, he had spoken critically about something he knew very little about, summarizing all "Oriental mysticism" as "simply more or less useless" to a Christian.[6] Only fifteen years later, he would begin to learn and discover a genuine encounter with Eastern religious teachers and practices and come to different conclusions. It is fascinating to me that his readers were willing—and are still willing—to make this journey with him. I think this is because we sense the genuine honesty in both the earlier blunders and arrogance and the later enlightenments.

"May I not come back without having settled the great affair. And found also the great compassion," he wrote in his journal two months before he died, speaking mysteriously about himself on the cusp of the tremendous 1968 trip to Asia. He was then fifty-three. What "great affair"? It was the love that he desired, which was ultimately the Love of God, and which in the final stages of his life was not found solely in his Christianity.

"You cannot rely on structures," he said in that final talk in Bangkok, just a few hours before his accidental death. He meant no monk, no Christian or other religious person, can assume that the structures—ecclesiastical, political, societal—that currently sustain their physical existence will exist or serve them in the future. He'd seen what happened to the Dalai Lama in Tibet. But, coming from the Trappist who loved organized religion, this was a difficult message for some to hear.

His note about settling the "great affair" inside himself was written on October 15, 1968, as he was leaving by plane from San Francisco, bound for Honolulu, then on to Bangkok. There was something about leaving for the East, after all those years studying Buddhism and Taoism and Hinduism, talking about Zen and practicing its arts, living as a Zen Catholic in his hermitage, that he had to see and experience it all on its home ground. "I am going home, to the home where I have never been in this body, where I have never been in this washable suit," he continued to write that day on the plane after takeoff.

His interest in going to Bangkok was also heightened by the war in Vietnam and the wound that the conflict was placing on the world, particularly Southeast Asia.[7] He'd been at the center of anti-war discussions in the church for several years, and he was exhausted by it.

The order that he found behind monastery gates, with certainty of conviction, was burst open when he began to encounter (not simply *read*) the spiritual masters of the East. When he faced living examples of contemplative living, everything he knew only in his head flew out the window like so many birds. All the evil and foreignness that he had once seen and felt in "the world," transformed in his spiritual experience. The badness of the world, and the problems within himself, and the past and present and future, he began to understand as one—part of the will of God and the movement of God.

Such a reading of the spiritual life is most fully present in Merton's great little book from 1965, *The Way of Chuang Tzu.* In the preface, he mysteriously says that the right way of life in the world should never be to try finding a way "out" of the world, but also that "Chuang Tzu [a Chinese philosopher from before the time of Christ] would have agreed with St. John of the Cross, that you enter upon this way when you leave all ways and, in some sense, get lost."[8]

In those last years of Merton's life, he was becoming willing and able to live in the mystery of things, finding God in the questions that are without answers. The religions of the East taught him this, and then he went back and found the same teachings in the Catholic spiritual tradition.

Dissolution of old orders and ways of doing things was seen by him as good and disrupting of established ways of doing things that don't work—old ways of thinking that bring people into conflict, to hate, to war, to misunderstanding—were dismantled in his late work. He didn't offer precise answers to problems, and this also upset some of his readers.

His final year or two would confuse many who knew him, and many more who simply read him. Why was Merton so personally and spiritually fulfilled by his encounter with other religious traditions, most of all Hinduism and Buddhism, on his final trip to Asia?

He was a man of the Second Vatican Council. Not present in Rome for that historic gathering, his ideas were nevertheless carried there in the persons of many of the gathered bishops. And perhaps the most important declaration to emerge from the council, *Nostra Aetate,* on how the Catholic Church relates to non-Christian religious traditions, was directly in line with Merton's thinking, as well as all his instincts and emotion. Ratified overwhelmingly by the bishops in 1965, it famously reads:

> *The Catholic Church rejects nothing that is true and holy in these religions. She regards with sincere reverence those ways of conduct and of life, those precepts and teachings, which though different in many aspects from the ones she holds and sets forth, nonetheless often reflect a ray of truth which enlightens all men.*

Thus, he wrote this in his final journal, from Asia, "I know and have seen what I was obscurely looking for."[9]

This was an affirmation that what he suspected was true, that what he was encountering in the great religious traditions of the East was, like his Catholicism, "true and holy." It all, in fact, felt true when he experienced it in person, and fed his enlightenment. He filled the pages of his last journals with all of this, and we'll never know where it might have taken him.

7

Creating Monastic Spirituality
for Everyone

"What is written about prayer in these pages is written primarily for monks."[1]

Merton knew that these words, written in his final year, were not really true. He went on to add that what he had to say about prayer was likely to be of interest to many people, monastic or not. This was his great gift: reaching into the monastic life of prayer and pulling its fruits and practices out for all to use. And doing so without losing any of the majesty and mystery!

He pointed toward monastic spiritual gifts for ordinary people. He showed us that it is possible to do what monks do, and to attain what monks are reaching for, while having jobs, families, and busy lives. He wrote about monastic spirituality with such hope and promise and confidence that we feel we can do it, too.

For example, he said in *The Silent Life:*

The world . . . has forgotten the joys of silence, the peace of solitude which is necessary, to some extent, for the fullness of

human living. Not all . . . are called to be hermits, but all . . .
need enough silence and solitude in their lives to enable the
deep inner voice of their own true self to be heard at least
occasionally.[2]

Him and me. Every one of us. A monk in Kentucky, a writer in
Milwaukee with a wife and four kids, or a barista in Seattle. All
of us.

To truly appreciate this openness and hopefulness, you have
to realize that even today—and especially in Merton's time
(those words were written nearly seventy-five years ago)—it's
common for religious people to believe that vowed religious
life creates a different kind of person, set apart. An "ontological
change" occurs at ordination, many in the clergy and religious
orders are taught, and believe. These ideas go back to the early
Middle Ages and were reinforced by church hierarchy whenever
the laity would begin to suggest that they, too, by virtue of the
sacrament of baptism, had full access to the Holy Spirit.

Merton began his monastic life believing that monks like him
were almost "a different species of being, pseudoangels . . . of
interior life."[3] It may be difficult for you to imagine thinking
such a thing today, but it's still common.

Not long ago, I encouraged a monastic writer I was editing
to remove paragraphs from his book in which he spoke of the
"essential difference" between those who take religious vows and
those who live "secular" lives. He was writing on the topic of
vocation and bemoaning the fact that more people don't see the
extraordinary blessing that comes only through a vocation to
vowed religious life. With a little prodding, he took my advice

and rewrote the chapter to say that every person has an equal vocation before God. I got the impression that he hadn't considered this point since he'd been in the seminary.

Another monastic writer recently explained:

> When I came to the monastery forty-six years ago, I was told that I was entering "the state of perfection." I wondered what that meant because I saw so much imperfection all around me. We no longer talk like that.[4]

Merton was embarrassed later to have thought it. The novelist Mary Gordon has recently reflected on this and on the astounding success of *The Seven Storey Mountain,* saying, "I am puzzled by the fact that more readers didn't find Merton's hatred for secular life so much a turnoff that they didn't finish the book. Or did they just skip the nasty bits, luxuriating in the monastic romance that it would take the author a decade to modify?"[5]

More than a decade after his monastic vocation began, he began writing, speaking, and working as an activist to say that a monk has a reciprocal relationship with the world he has left behind. His freedom to leave the world—in terms of its expectations of what makes for a useful life—is for the purpose of helping to free that world of those expectations (and those constraints!).[6] In other words, *monk* becomes much more broadly defined.

Who is a monk, then, but one who turns away from the world's expectations and gives of themselves fully to God, practicing daily prayer, contemplation, concentration upon scriptures, and the works of mercy and faithfulness that mark people as God's own.

Culminating in the Fourth and Walnut experience, when he suddenly saw all the people on the street corner in the shopping district of downtown Louisville as his brothers and sisters, on the same pilgrimage that he was on, Merton became a spiritual teacher who set out to learn from others more than teach them what he already understood.

SOLITUDE IN COMMON

He was uniquely positioned to do all of this. And then he didn't live long enough to see what we would do with it.

On the mountain of his hermitage, Merton was able to do what he did because down below in the valley was a monastery of 150 monks praying the hours. Regular confession. Obedience to an abbot, even and especially at his craziest moments, he was grounded and girded. We now live in a time of consuming spirituality in a series of disconnected events. We have self-proclaimed hermits who are really just introverts or, worse, misanthropes. We even have virtual communion in places. And there is Merton himself, at the end of his life declaring that we no longer should rely on structures. This was easier for him to say than for us to do, because he had been deeply formed by structures. It can be a mistake for those who want to be formed by someone like Thomas Merton to think that they can do so without any of the religious disciplines and vows that formed him.

One of Merton's novices, Br. Paul Quenon, followed in his teacher's steps in many ways. He became a monk at Gethsemani after being inspired from reading *The Seven Storey Mountain*.

Then he became a poet and a photographer, just as his former
novice master had been. Today, Br. Paul articulates Merton's
message in a way that, I suspect, Merton would have done if
he'd lived longer. Br. Paul speaks in his memoir of gladly and
purposefully living a "useless life." What is that, exactly? "[A]n
emptying out of the clutter within the mind and heart . . . to
make room for God."[7]

In an essay for *Commonweal* magazine in 1966 about contemplatives needing to live in, and not apart from, the world,
Merton admitted:

> *Is the world a problem? . . . Perhaps . . . I am personally in-*
> *volved in the absurdity of the question; due to a book I wrote*
> *thirty years ago, I have myself become a sort of stereotype of*
> *the world-denying contemplative—the man who spurned New*
> *York, spat on Chicago, and tromped on Louisville, heading for*
> *the woods with Thoreau in one pocket, John of the Cross*
> *in another, and holding the Bible open at the Apocalypse.*
> *This personal stereotype is probably my own fault, and it is*
> *something I have to try to demolish.*[8]

He was exaggerating to make a point. He hadn't written the book
thirty years earlier, but only twenty. He was anxious to disown
it. Merton began to see that his life—including and especially
his monastic life, for that was his first vocation—was not for
himself. He wrote:

> *Solitude has its own special work: a deepening awareness that*
> *the world needs. A struggle against alienation. True solitude is*

*deeply aware of the world's needs. It does not hold the world
at arm's length.*[9]

At about the same time, he also wrote this, a lesson he gradually learned over time: "True solitude is not mere separateness.
It tends only to *unity*."[10]

You don't have to be living in a cloister to live that vocation.
And you can't remain entirely alone if you truly live it. Merton
knew this and opened new pathways to religious life that have
become more and more common in the decades since his death
in 1968.

Other spiritual teachers, following Merton's lead, have
demonstrated since his time how to live as a monk in the midst
of everyday life. There is Christine Valters Paintner, an American living in Ireland, who created the online community known
as Abbey of the Arts—a monastery for people who might never
leave home to visit. From there, she teaches daily courses on
topics such as *The Soul's Slow Ripening,* and *Earth, Our Original
Monastery.* These are also book titles of hers. She recognizes
Merton as an inspiration for her work, saying something that
we said already above: "The root of the word monk is *monachos*
which means single, as in singular of focus, or single-hearted. The
monk seeks to discover the divine presence in everything, every
moment, every person. This is, of course, a lifelong practice and
is never 'perfected.'"[11]

Merton's most notable heir is probably Fr. Richard Rohr.
A Franciscan friar and Catholic priest, Rohr is not often identified with those titles today. He has instead become the go-to
teacher of contemplative—mostly Christian, but not exclusively—

wisdom. Primarily from his home at the Center for Action and Contemplation in New Mexico, which he founded, Rohr teaches the necessity of a contemplative approach to the world: not accepting it on face value; it will deceive you; but not rejecting the world as bad or wrong either, because "every creature is a word of God," as he often puts it.

A student of Merton's, Rohr pleads with people: "Why, oh why, do Christians allow these temporary costumes, or what Thomas Merton called the 'false self,' to pass for the substantial self, which is always 'hidden with Christ in God.'"[12] And the true self that each person must find—and are able to discover inside of them—doesn't have to be Christian. God is love, and love is God wherever it be found.

If Merton had lived another fifty or sixty years, I suspect that he would have taken his readers to places similar to those where Paul Quenon, Christian Valters Paintner, and Richard Rohr now take them.

Toward the end of his life, Merton wrote:

> We have not yet rediscovered the primary usefulness of the useless. From this loss of all sense of being, all capacity to live for the sake of living and praising God, all thankfulness, all "Eucharistic" spirit, comes the awful frustrated restlessness of our world obsessed with "doing" so that even "having fun" becomes a job of work.[13]

And "We must learn to realize that the love of God seeks us in every situation, and seeks our good. His inscrutable love seeks our awakening."[14]

ALL ABOUT FRIENDSHIP

The last decade saw Merton increasingly sense the monk's vocation in friendship, reaching out to people across divides, and
even influencing world events. He sought to correspond from his
cloister and hermitage with dissidents, poets, and intellectuals
who were at the forefront of political and social change. For
example, deeply affected after reading Boris Pasternak's *Doctor
Zhivago,* Merton wrote the Russian a letter. Soon, the two were
corresponding regularly, sending and receiving letters through
third parties, since Pasternak was under the careful watch of his
Soviet handlers.

Some of the free spirits and rebels who appealed to Merton
were also creatives naturally drawn to an unusual monk and
his ideas. They also sometimes encouraged Merton's restlessness
and rebelliousness. Most prominent of these was the Nicaraguan
poet and politician Ernesto Cardenal, who recently died in 2020.
Cardenal became a novice at Gethsemani under Merton, left two
years later, and tried for years after that to convince his spiritual
father to leave Gethsemani and join him in Latin America. There
were others, too, who understood the restless contemplative in
Fr. Louis and tried to "help" him away. But Merton's place was
at his monastery. He was able to combine in himself a free spirit
that challenged authority and yet remained true to it.

He was corresponding with Dorothy Day, as well, encouraging her radical work in the Catholic Church as an advocate for
the poor, undisturbed by those who accused her prophetic voice
as being too socialist or too political. It was simply the politics
of Jesus. "I am certainly with you," Merton told Day in 1959.[15]

To the great Jesuit anti-war activist Daniel Berrigan, SJ, Merton wrote before Berrigan had ever been arrested, "I am very glad to hear that the Pax movement is getting started in this country and that you are part of it. So am I."[16] That was November 1961. Three years later, Merton would host Berrigan and eight others for an activists' summit at the monastery in Kentucky—during the time period when his religious superiors insisted, by the vow of obedience, that Merton not publish articles of a political nature.

A collection of letters of this sort from this time in his life came to be called the *Cold War Letters*. Long before they were formally published, Merton mimeographed and distributed copies all over the world to friends. In Cold War Letter 61, he wrote to a then very young James Forest, who already knew what it was like to protest and get arrested: "The peace movement needs more than zeal. It . . . needs to be organized . . . and it is necessary for the people to . . . be formed into a coherent nucleus."[17] Fr. Louis thought he could help. He would be a grounding point for many. This was his prophetic work.

Then he was inspired in April 1963 by the marches and arrests of civil rights workers, clergy black and white, in Alabama, and the incarceration of Martin Luther King Jr. in Birmingham, followed by King's poignant "Letter from Birmingham Jail," portions of which were first published a month later in the *New York Post Sunday Magazine*. Clearly working through his own issues of participation in the struggle, and as a challenge to others on some form of the sidelines, Merton wrote his own "Letters to a White Liberal." It holds up today as relevant and timely, even sixty years later.

He challenges whites who talk about wanting change but are unwilling to sacrifice their position to achieve it. Speaking of civil rights, he says that blacks look upon the white liberal this way:

> *He . . . knows . . . that your material comforts, your security, and your congenial relations with the establishment are much more important to you than your rather volatile idealism, and that when the game gets rough you will be quick to see your own interests menaced by his demands.*[18]

On matters of race and inequality, Merton's influence wasn't only felt among whites—whom he was attempting to convince of their privilege, and the necessity of whites standing with blacks to demand their full rights as human beings and citizens. Merton was read and appreciated by many African Americans at that time, too. The Black Panther Eldridge Cleaver, for instance, told audiences that Merton's remarks on the vitality of life in Harlem and his witness to the bigotry of white Christians inspired him. It was Cleaver who also said, "You either have to be part of the solution, or you're going to be part of the problem." He knew that Merton was part of the solution, and he called him "brother."[19]

Merton was also soon speaking out directly against the American war in Vietnam, first through a letter to the editor published in the magazine *Commonweal* (February 1965).[20]

But there were some who criticized him for attempting to speak prophetically and polemically from behind the walls of a monastery. The prominent church historian and public theologian Martin Marty was one such critic. Reviewing *Seeds of Destruc-*

tion—in which "Letters to a White Liberal" first appeared—
for the *New York Herald Tribune,* Marty resented a monk who
wasn't "on the ground" in the fight for civil rights or in the
anti-war effort and yet speaking as if he had authority on such
matters. Marty also resented the monk challenging the motives
of white liberals, for he was one of them—who were on the
front lines at marches, sit-ins, and other dangerous places.

Two years later, the feminist theologian Rosemary Radford
Ruether, who was also immersed in the civil rights struggle,
protesting beside blacks and teaching at a predominantly African American university (Howard), initiated a contentious correspondence with Merton along similar lines: criticizing him for
talking and writing about action instead of acting. Unlike Marty,
Ruether was a Catholic, but she, too, had little patience for a
monk speaking authoritatively from behind walls.

Perhaps it's no accident, then, that Fr. Louis's final talk (with
which this book began) was on the subject of how monasticism
and Marxism might work together. He was not defensive on these
matters; he never seems to have seriously questioned his calling
to be a monk; but he was, to the end, earnestly trying to figure
out his role in world events as a contemplative. Every would-be
monk and contemplative still has to wrestle with this tension.

Another friend from this time was the folk singer and famous
anti-war protester Joan Baez. She remembered: "I first heard of
Thomas Merton in the way names were kicked around in the
1960s when we were looking for cohorts and were just a ragged
bunch of outcasts most people thought were nuts. . . . [S]ome-
body told me about this Trappist monk who was an outspoken
antiwar activist—or at least as active as he could be in his

confines." She adds, "I don't think I was invited to Gethsemani—
I think I probably invited myself."[21] She visited him there at the
end of 1966.

. . .

Given all this outward-focused energy, it feels inevitable that
Merton began to desire to leave Kentucky, feeling that he
couldn't be who he was supposed to be within its confines. In
1959, he petitioned the Vatican to leave Gethsemani and the
Trappists, but with a desire to remain a monk by moving outside the United States. He had his eye on his former novice
Ernesto Cardenal and the experiential, contemplative, monastic-
political enterprise Cardenal founded in Nicaragua after leaving
Gethsemani.

Merton's abbot, James Fox, however, quickly traveled to
Rome and met with the curia to squash the petition. Six years
later, he would seriously contemplate the request once again,
even writing letters that Cardenal, who was then an ordained
secular priest, might mail to the Vatican on his behalf. But that
time never came. Merton never instructed Cardenal to mail those
letters—that second request.[22]

For all these reasons, Merton remains a signal figure for those
of us who feel that we have found our vocation, but then face
obstacles in that vocation or questions as to how to work it out
in the day-to-day. He was passionate, but he was patient.

Abbot James Fox steadfastly refused to relax the ways of Trappist cenobitic monasticism for the sake of his one loquacious
monk. But, in January 1968, Fox retired, and his replacement
was open to change. Soon, Merton was confirming by letter that

he would be allowed to leave the monastery for a very long trip later that year to visit friends in East Asia, including the Dalai Lama in the Himalayas, to visit Buddhist temples and shrines in Japan, and to attend an East-West monastic conference in Bangkok.

8

Leaving Sainthood Behind

"This inner 'I,' which is always alone, is always universal: for in this inmost 'I' my own solitude meets the solitude of every other [person] and the solitude of God" (*Disputed Questions*).[1]

This is an example of Merton's teachings that most endure, with universal relevance, but that also point to why he will never be as popular with sainthood committees as he is with spiritual pilgrims looking for lanterns to carry them through the night. For many Catholics, Merton wasn't Catholic enough.

He learned from a Chinese scholar, Dr. John C. H. Wu, that his name in Chinese meant "Silent Lamp." In fact, that is the title of one of the best biographies of Merton (see "Suggestions for Further Reading"). It also points to who he was and who he remains. His gift to us includes providing a vision for life as a gift of God, and of God as light to see, and as breath to give life. This came at a time in the popular imagination—which is still with us—when old models of God were drying and dying.

It was April 8, 1966, when *Time* magazine, then a mainstay in homes across the United States, ran a feature story that was boldly titled in big red block letters against a black background sprawled across the front cover: "IS GOD DEAD?" Merton's life said no, and showed a way forward. He wrote:

> *God is not a "problem" and we who live the contemplative life have learned by experience that one cannot know God as long as one seeks to solve "the problem of God."*[2]

As I mentioned in the introduction, Pope Francis addressed a joint session of the U.S. Congress in September 2015 and praised four exemplary Americans from history: Abraham Lincoln, Martin Luther King Jr., Dorothy Day, and Thomas Merton. The pope called Merton "above all a man of prayer" and "also a man of dialogue, a promoter of peace between peoples and religions." I learned a few years later over dinner with Rabbi Abraham Skorka, one of Pope Francis's best friends from Buenos Aires, that Skorka had emailed his old friend several quotations from Merton in the couple of months before the pope's speech. It is interesting—and telling—that a rabbi might have helped to spark an interest in Thomas Merton on the part of the Holy Roman pontiff!

About that night when Pope Francis recommended Merton before an audience of hundreds of millions of people—I remember it well. It was notable, in particular, because Merton had never been a favorite of popes or the papal curia. He had subverted Vatican authority when he was forbidden to speak and write on politics during the Cold War and nevertheless found ways to circulate his *Cold War Letters* and other writings in the last decade of his life that made the censors nervous.

As Merton entered his fifties and his political activity increased, he also found creative ways to avoid those censors. He was known on occasion not to send an article to them by utilizing a provision that said if the publication was of limited circulation, then the censorship process was unnecessary. A censor's job is to help the author and religious order avoid controversy. Their mandate includes looking for theological error (which is what the *Nihil obstat,* meaning "Nothing hinders," printed on the copyright page of a book declares). But beyond that, censors often would go to matters of propriety. For this reason, censors' judgments would vary widely from one to another. And an author might dread a particular censor in the same way a trial attorney dreads facing a certain judge based on a reputation for severity. Merton at times bent that rule almost to a breaking point.

Merton began to see his writing as much more for everyday folks, not for satisfying religious authorities. As a contemplative, and the most popular Catholic spiritual writer of his time, he showed people how to become contemplatives. Then he realized that a life of contemplation could not mean a life apart from the turmoil and troubles of the world. In his writing, this began with a provocative and stunning poem entitled "Chant to Be Used in Processions Around a Site with Furnaces." In the words of the best interpreter of his poems, it "deals with the tragedy of Auschwitz and proceeds in the manner of a monotone recording of flat statements spoken by a commander in charge of a gas chamber. Each horror is recorded in unfeeling, mechanical recitative."[3] It first appeared in *The Catholic Worker,* the prophetic publication founded by Dorothy Day—and shocked many readers of his spirituality books.

This, in turn, inaugurated a whole new aspect to Merton's reputation. He went on to protest and indict other human atrocities, the business of nuclear arms proliferation, and the willingness of Christians to accommodate the murderous justification of these evil creations, to name a few. The first Cold War Letter, in 1961, stated:

> *This is purely and simply the crucifixion over again. Those who think there can be a just cause for measures that gravely risk leading to the destruction of the entire human race are in the most dangerous illusion.*

He goes on to add, "The extent of our spiritual obtuseness is reaching a frightful scale."[4]

He wasn't referring to people generally but implicitly also to the Catholic hierarchy, which was deafeningly silent on these issues. Catholic bishops are rarely prophetic. They tend to "wait and see," and this frustrated Merton. There were also prominent American Catholics who actively supported the Cold War policies of their government leaders. Senator Joseph McCarthy of Wisconsin, from the 1950s, is too easy of an example. There were also the subtler and more persuasive William F. Buckley Jr., founder of the *National Review,* and Clare Boothe Luce, a former U.S. ambassador, as well as a friend to the Abbey of Gethsemani and early supporter of Merton's, who in the years after Fidel Castro's revolution in Cuba counted among her close friends archconservatives Barry Goldwater and Ronald Reagan.[5]

Within a year of this activity, Merton was silenced by his superiors and told to stop writing such things. But he kept on writing, circulating them privately, knowing full well that his friends would send them to more friends, and so on. One friend from that time, James W. Douglass, summarized, "Merton is trying to call forth the saving presence of God . . . needed to save us from our own violence."[6] Many in the church hierarchy were unwilling to follow him there, and that explains a lot of why Pope Francis's affirmation of the monk in 2015 surprised so many of us.

Two other reasons predominate for why Merton has not always been recommended as safe and holy for the faithful. First, there is the matter of his love affair with Margie. Because of that indiscretion, there was this disapproval: "In 2005, the editors of the *United States Catholic Catechism for Adults* planned to feature stories of prominent American Catholics. Initially, Merton was included among other noteworthies, until some high-profile Catholics opposed the move. Bowing to pressure, the editors expunged him."[7]

HIS OTHER WEAKNESSES

There are also other concerns about Merton's possible sainthood relating to his personal conduct. He could at times be reckless.

His journal for April 6, 1968, for instance, records the following weekend spent at the monastery, in his hermitage, in Bardstown bars, and at a friend's home. This all took place over a twenty-four-hour period on the Saturday before Holy Week.

"I went out to the Gatehouse where four college girls from St. Louis were waiting for me." He'd arranged to meet them. They wanted an interview. He says that their tape recorder broke down, "So I took them up to the hermitage to record on mine." Surely his abbot, and any other Trappist then or now, would have thought more carefully about meeting alone with four young women. Then, "As we made the tape we drank beer." One of the young women "asked a lot of leading questions . . . [on] premarital sex, etc." He should have at least wrapped things up then. They finished the interview in the hermitage and then got in their car and drove to Bardstown to a restaurant and bar where, Merton says, "I got a bottle of bourbon and we made a night of it." Then they went to another bar "and we drank some more whiskey."[8]

He went to sleep in the hermitage, alone, but after seeing the four young women again the following day (over mass, then breakfast), he records a measure of sexual frustration in his journal. He didn't ask his abbot's permission to have these meetings with the young women. Permission surely wouldn't have been granted. But he returns to his senses, and he has the monastic life of stability of obedience to ground him.

I have heard Trappists say that the essence of their vocation is simply that they stay put. Not religion or faith or prayer but staying where they promised to stay until death is what most defines them.

He probably too easily noticed the beauty of women. His adjective for young women is often "pretty." For example, there are two strangers he observes in his journal—"pretty Swedish girl," and "pretty Thai girl," in the Bangkok airport on October 18, 1968. Also that day, there were "utterly lovely—and haughty—Indian girls" in the jottings of what he saw.[9] Thirty years earlier, as a graduate student, he'd written in letters to his friend Robert Lax certain crudities of expression that are usually reserved for adolescents and early teenagers—but these expressions from 1968 were from the latest stage in his life: the mature Merton.

A therapist might look on this and see a man who is still searching for his lost mother. Merton is like other great creatives, his contemporary Pablo Neruda, for instance, who wrote so many beautiful love poems, starting at the age of sixteen, perhaps in part to make up for the loss of his mother's love. Neruda's mother died in childbirth, when Neruda was born. Remember, Merton's mother died when he was six.

FORGET SAINTHOOD

But the most important reason why Merton will never be a saint is also the reason why he is the most important Catholic religious figure of the second half of the twentieth century: he showed how to be in relationship with people of other religious and spiritual traditions, based on friendship, study, and prayer, demonstrating that kinship across religious boundaries is central to wrestling with God. He was dedicated to interfaith dialogue, and close friendships with people of non-Christian religious traditions, that still make some people uncomfortable. It seems that Christians will never agree on what is the proper balance between friendship and conversation with people of other faiths. In one of his last books, he wrote:

> [T]here is a monastic outlook which is common to all those who have elected to question the value of a life submitted entirely to arbitrary secular presuppositions, dictated by social convention, and dedicated to the pursuit of temporal satisfactions which are perhaps only a mirage. Whatever may be the value of "life in the world" there have been, in all cultures, men [and women] who have claimed to find something they vastly prefer in solitude.[10]

Not only had he matured in his understanding of what a monk is supposed to be, but he came to see that monks are first of all contemplatives, and contemplatives speak across the religious traditions to something core and central to being human before the Creator.

Merton's conversion toward interfaith dialogue and theological openness in many ways reflected the journey being undertaken by the whole Roman Catholic Church, which was leaning toward what would become landmark changes to its practice and teaching in documents such as *Nostra Aetate*. He lived to see some of the dramatic and positive reforms of his church, brought by Vatican II, and then he died long before the next two generations of leaders of his church pulled away from those same reforms. In many respects, Catholics are no closer to understanding today what Merton grasped sixty years ago.

So if 1958–1962 were the years when Merton began to use his influence to impact societal change, culminating in the *Cold War Letters,* the years 1963–1965 were when this aspect of his work deepened further, particularly on issues of race relations in the United States and the necessity of dialogue with other faiths. His conversations with representatives of other religious and spiritual traditions became extensive. It would have been a full-time job for most people with how often he was receiving visitors, writing letters, joining groups, and attempting to persuade people through articles and poems and every other means available to him. One small publisher in Kentucky today, whose series of books devoted to this aspect of Merton's life, almost tells the story simply by the book titles:

Merton and Indigenous Wisdom
Merton and Buddhism
Merton and the Protestant Tradition
Merton and the Tao
Merton and Judaism
Merton and Sufism
Merton and Hesychasm[11]

This is when he developed deep friendships with people whose names are often recognized—such as Thich Nhat Hanh, the Vietnamese Buddhist monk; His Holiness the Dalai Lama, leader of the Tibetan people in exile; D. T. Suzuki, renowned Japanese interpreter of Zen; and Rabbi Zalman Schachter (later Schachter-Shalomi), founder of the Jewish Renewal movement.

Thich Nhat Hanh remembered Merton this way: "[C]onversation with him was so easy. . . . He did not talk so much about himself. He was constantly asking questions. And then he would listen."[12]

These conversations took place primarily through letters, but also in personal visits, as religious leaders from around the world would go to Kentucky to see the Trappist monk.

For all these reasons, although he'll never be a saint, Merton remains a prophet.

. . .

Most of all, he remains a writer. To use psychologist Erik Erikson's terminology, Merton can be understood as undergoing many identity crises: as a son; as the rebellious one; as a pilgrim; as a monk—again the rebellious one. But he is probably best understood as a writer.

As one Merton interpreter has put it: "Merton's stability at Gethsemani for twenty-seven years was hard therapy for the wanderlust he had inherited from his father. Yet his monastic stability would become the great blessing for his writing, his teaching and his art."[13]

It is through his writing that he became himself and met the world. I do not know for certain if he met God through his pen—but I believe he did. I have known Trappists who speak of a "No-name Me"—the true, unique, and untouchable identity of each person known only to God. They pray to know this "No-name Me"—which usually takes place only in the quiet and dark of the soul. I know this probably sounds overly philosophical or metaphysical, and it is. But it also rings true. This is how Merton once explained it:

At the center of our being is a point of nothingness which is un-
touched by sin and by illusion, a point of pure truth, a point
or spark which belongs entirely to God, which is never at our
disposal, from which God disposes of our lives, which is inac-
cessible to the fantasies of our own mind or the brutalities of
our own will. This little point of nothingness and of absolute
poverty is the pure glory of God in us.[14]

For Merton, perhaps not. As he imagined his monastic life
about to begin, writing less than two weeks before leaving for
Kentucky, he reflected, somewhat dramatically:

There will be no more future, not in the world, not in geogra-
phy, not in travel, not in change, not in variety, conversa-
tions, new work, new problems in writing, new friends—none
of that, but a far better progress, all interior and quiet!!![15]

But to follow that thread is to see a tale of frustration and deny-
ing his dramatic self-denials. His writing—contrary to the ideals
of the young convert and monk—would become his conversion
and his charism.

How did Dom Frederic Dunne, his first abbot, know this?
We'll never know for sure. But he encouraged Merton to scribe
his conversion, to have a pen in his hand and his fingers on typewriter keys in the way that other monks were encouraged to
occupy themselves toward conversion via choir and the Daily
Office, or manual labor, or theological study, or silent prayer.
Merton was as loquacious as they come, and he was encouraged

not to be silent and not to forget himself behind those large monastery doors, but to write, to write, to write.

And so, in his fifties, two years before he died, he could finally realize who he was. I believe he found that elusive wholeness. It was true, and not self-deprecating, when he wrote in the preface to the 1966 Japanese translation of *The Seven Storey Mountain:*

> It is possible to doubt whether I have become a monk (a doubt I have to live with), but it is not possible to doubt that I am a writer, that I was born one and will most probably die as one.

This is something he would never have said—or could have known about himself—when he first entered the monastery.

Writers who're always writing about themselves—and Merton sometimes comes across this way—can be narcissistic. Sometimes the religious writer who does this can be the worst offender of all, because like Merton, they'll say things like this, as he wrote in a letter to his publisher Jay Laughlin in 1948: "I don't want to conceive myself in any way as having any kind of a mission in the world or the Church except to see God."

But such a writer may, in fact, be ego neutral. I believe we are drawn to reading Merton because of the ease with which we can see and feel his experiences. I think it's possible that when writing *The Seven Storey Mountain* and *The Sign of Jonas,* he was simply and honestly writing to please God. It wasn't saccharine. It wasn't untrue. His explanation of motivation to an old friend supports this: "I don't know what audience I might have been thinking of. I suppose I just put down what was in me, under the eyes of God who knows what is in me."[16] I think these words have to be taken for their simple truth. I suggest that readers' enthusiasm for Merton's writing generally was and is an attunement to a sort of purity in the author's intentions. In that same purity, Merton wrote in another letter to a publisher-friend, just as *The Seven Storey Mountain* was about to release:

> *I don't think work is as important as any of us feel it to be when the mood is upon us. Cultivate tranquility—detachment—the purity of heart that does things simply to please God.*[17]

That's what I find in him.

9

We Are All Secrets

We have come full circle, back to where chapter 1 began. We are again back in Bangkok, at the end of Merton's last long leg of his pilgrimage. He has sat with the Dalai Lama; he has wondered at the Buddhas of Sri Lanka; he has continued, to the last, to imagine a quieter place where he might pray, wondering, if he ever could stop writing.

There was almost no end to what he wanted to absorb, grasp, and contemplate. His subjects often came out of him as "causes": Native American rights, civil rights for African Americans, protesting the war in Vietnam, and so on. But the curiosity is also revealed in the astounding range of people around the world with whom he actively corresponded. Despite his abbot frequently encouraging him to reduce the number of contacts he maintained outside the monastery, and to write fewer letters, Merton kept on at a pace that would be unusual for anyone. He was constantly trying to learn, and he teaches us to do the same. To be endlessly curious and always ready to listen to another's truth.

I think that Merton came to see that every person is a puzzle, and as he grew older, the depth of the puzzle of each person became more and more mysterious. "We are all secrets," he jotted quietly in his journal in 1968, four months before his Asia trip. This is wisdom that comes with age.

Also with age, and as a sort of cumulation of curiosity, he reached a point of exhaustion combined with a desire for what Christian mystics have sometimes called *absorption in the Divine*. Whether he could have ever entered the wordless state that he seems to have longed for in the last year of his life, we will never know. But he was headed in that direction.

On that trip, beyond Bangkok, he had planned to speak to Trappist and other monastic communities in Indonesia and near Hong Kong. Before leaving for Asia, he'd given a retreat at a monastery in California, and with the blessing of his abbot, had taken short trips within the state to look at possible sites for a long-term hermitage solution to his desire for quiet. But I don't think he was being honest with himself when he wrote this in his journal two months before leaving for Asia. He was ruminating again about his desire for solitude, knowing that his new abbot, Fr. Flavian Burns (elected in January 1968), seemed open to helping him find a more remote hermitage:

In eight weeks I am to leave here. And who knows—I may not come back. On an evening like this the place is certainly beautiful—but you can seldom count on it really being quiet (though it is at the moment). Traffic on the road. Kids at the lake. Guns. Machines, and Boone's dog yelling in the wood at night. And people coming all the time. All this is to be ex-

*pected and I don't complain of it. But if I can find somewhere
to disappear to, I will. And if I am to begin a relatively wandering life with no fixed abode, that's all right too.*[1]

This is how his final half year of life looks. . . .

Starting May 6, Merton begins a seven-month period of travel
and pilgrimage that will end in his death in Thailand. For much
of May, he is in California and New Mexico visiting other monastic communities and seeking that new location for his eremitic
vocation. June, July, and August, he's back at Gethsemani, but
then leaves again on September 11, first returning to New Mexico, then to Alaska, where he's also looking for remote locations to relocate. A month in Alaska is followed by a few days in
San Francisco (there's a humorous episode of the monk people-
watching with beat poet and publisher Lawrence Ferlinghetti),
before his flight to Calcutta. There, he speaks at a conference
and meets Chögyam Trungpa Rinpoche, a then-young Tibetan
Buddhist teacher, who later recalls, "He was the first genuine
person I met from the West."[2] Then to New Delhi, followed by
a month in the Himalayas, including several meetings with the
Dalai Lama.

Finally, Sri Lanka (then known as Ceylon), where he stands
in awe before massive stone statues of the Buddha—and writes
about and photographs them in what becomes, after his death,
The Asian Journal of Thomas Merton. Then, he makes his way to
Bangkok, where chapter 1 of this book began.

He says in one of the early talks he gives in Asia in those final
months, "My dear brothers [and sisters], we are already one. But
we imagine that we are not."[3]

. . .

Reflecting on this extraordinary monk's life, to this point, I think most readers will begin to see that even a spiritual adept like Thomas Merton can sometimes know what is good for him without consistently following it. There is a strand of interpretation that suggests this, and that the trip to Asia was the final straw. That somehow all that he was pursuing on his Asia trip was the anticipated true moment when Merton would finally seek and find and remain faithful to the solitude which he sought. I don't think we could ever know this to be true. I think it was the final straw only by accident, or providence, because Merton happened to die there. That same strand of interpretation then suggests that his death was itself the final unity and silence he so craved, but that is too mystical an understanding for a biographical work such as this.

There is nothing in his experience up to that point to suggest that he wouldn't have relocated to another remoter hermitage location, whether in the mountains of California, the wilds of Alaska, or the forests of Indonesia, and then remained as loquacious as he had always been, receiving guests, dancing at picnics, investigating whatever stimulated his mind, corresponding with rebels and saints all over the world. But that's okay. "We are all secrets."

A QUESTION OF FAITHFULNESS

Many of his fellow Catholics have worried about Merton's fidelity to the faith, given what he wrote in his final year and his mysterious death in East Asia. *The Asian Journal,* published a few years after his death, confused some while inspiring others. There was this passage, for instance:

> Last night I dreamed I was, temporarily, back at Gethsemani.
> I was dressed in a Buddhist monk's habit, but with more black
> and red and gold, a "Zen habit," in color more Tibetan than
> Zen . . . I met some women in the corridor, visitors and stu-
> dents of Asian religion, to whom I was explaining I was a
> kind of Zen monk and Gelugpa together, when I woke up.[4]

Then, when the other private journals began to appear in print, after a lengthy period of time when Merton's will forbade their publication, the details about "M" and other episodes and comments of naked honesty again revealed how the monk continued to evolve, struggle, learn, and grow. But in the minds of those who want mostly to revere their spiritual teachers, this, too, proved troubling.

And then there is that honest and serious way that his attention was divided in so many directions, soon after his fame made the monastery experience less compelling for him. We saw this in earlier chapters. Paul Pearson, director of the Thomas Merton Center at Bellarmine University, has estimated that this cloistered/solitude-loving monk corresponded with 2,100 people in the five years alone between 1963 until his death.[5] I find it extraordinary, given such evidence, that Merton commentators have often taken a defensive tone to defend Merton's extraordinary activities, as if it weren't unusual for a monk of any era.

Within two decades of his death, inter-spiritual pioneers who learned much from him, such as Wayne Teasdale and Raimon

Panikkar, could speak of being "monks in the world"—and it would make perfect sense to us. Panikkar wrote, "I speak of an inspiration and an urge." For him, monasticism and monasteries were no longer the point of relevancy. Instead, "[a monk] is the person who aspires to reach the ultimate goal of life with all his being by renouncing all that is not necessary to it."[6]

Merton is the one who led us there. His beautiful 1957 book, *The Silent Life*, begins by saying, "A monk is a man who has been called by the Holy Spirit to relinquish the cares, desires and ambitions of other men, and devote his entire life to seeking God."[7] Rightly or wrongly, we interpret those lines now to mean that one doesn't have to take vows in a monastery to be a monk.

In his last year, he even mentions in his journal a conversation with three young men—two African American, one white—who were visiting Gethsemani from the inner city of Cleveland. They talked about meditation and the death of Dr. King, and Merton records one of them saying that day that, in Cleveland, they are "living like monks" together.[8]

No longer does the work one does from day-to-day matter so much in being this kind of monk, as does the intentions of desire and devotion that Merton mentions. Being a monk is a values-driven, practice-driven enterprise, and it is often attempted outside a cloister or religious community. Still, something, or some things, are usually lost in the transition. In this new fashioning, monks become part-time, or worse, being monk-like becomes a kind of hobby or fashion. Given the difficulties that the church has been through—scandals, abuses, and infighting—the role of the traditional monk, like that of a priest, is no longer as an icon of spiritual living the way it once was. But being a monk is still aspirational, and this is largely thanks to Thomas Merton. Very little in religious life is in fact as aspirational as this is.

Also in *The Silent Life,* he appeals universally to anyone and everyone who aspires to make a serious commitment to become a contemplative. Even when he offers details about Carthusian spiritual practice (offering greater solitude for hermits than Trappist life), it sounds as if it is something you and I can do ourselves, right where we are:

> *The real "cell" is a bedroom and sitting room with two alcoves, one an oratory and the other a study. In the one the monk kneels in meditation or recites the day hours of the canonical office with all the ceremonies that are performed when the monks are together in choir. In the other he has his desk, a shelf of books—the Bible, a volume or two of the Fathers, or some theology, [and] some favorite spiritual reading.*[9]

For this reason, and because he saw how contemplation relates to activism, the civil rights activist Julius Lester wrote in 1971:

> *The politics of confrontation is being replaced by a politic strangely akin to the essence of monasticism. The first person to recognize this was Thomas Merton, the Trappist monk who died in 1968; he saw in the youth culture "an attitude toward the world which is analogous to that of the monk."*[10]

MAKE YOUR SILENCE USEFUL

"Snowflakes meet on the pages of the Breviary," Merton wrote in a journal entry on February 29, 1968, the final year of his life. He was by himself a great deal, having achieved what he'd long sought: a permanent hermitage.

He had come to realize that his silence was not for himself and was not solely for the purpose of deepening his relationship with God. His solitude would enable him to fight for the spiritual lives of others. So he became a champion of imprisoned authors, anti-war activists, Catholic Worker volunteers, discarded poets, and spiritually aspiring people everywhere who filled his hermitage front porch with correspondence. In *The Seven Storey Mountain,* he had contrasted the "miserable, noisy cruel earth" with "the marvelous joy of silence and solitude."[11] But now he came to fully engage with the crises of the world. He is in dialogue with the world, not preaching to it.

What he discovered over the course of a decades-long struggle with silence in his life was how it couldn't—or shouldn't ever—be an end in itself. Silence, for him, was put to use. Silence refit him for living more contemplatively, with greater wisdom; he was able to reenter the world to help redeem it only after having left the world's noise behind. Daily. So he wrote: "[T]his silence that enfolded me, spoke to me, and spoke louder and more eloquently than any voice."[12]

But where will we find this kind of silence and sustain it, in our lives—we who don't have the benefit of a daily monastic routine or environment? Some small measure of outer silence is essential if we are to discover our inner silence.

The wrong use of silence leads to anger, fear, or depression. I know this in my own life. I'll mention two experiences, one on a larger scale, one smaller. The larger: I lived for a decade in the Vermont woods in a log cabin on twenty acres of forest. We heated with wood, made trails on the mountain behind our house, and lived, as Thoreau said, "deliberately." It was quiet, but for me, it was a scene of the ending of an unhappy marriage in which that silence allowed us to ignore our problems, go about our own work, and postpone the well-being that every person should enjoy. Now, the smaller-scale example: I work from home and have done so for going on twenty years. As a writer and editor, I work in silence much of the time. But I also find that too much silence can turn a good thing into bad. It can be a breeding ground for false ideas about myself or others—that's the anger. It can be a time when I don't have others around me to balance my feelings and challenge my ideas—and that can bring on fear and small-scale depression.

This leads to a related conclusion that is almost too simple to say out loud. We need to practice something to get better at it. Whether it's prayer or picketing, one doesn't simply pick up a breviary or a sign and do it well. Merton said in a letter to some friends near the end of his life, "Our real journey in life is interior; it is a matter of growth."[13]

BE A VOICE IN THE WILDERNESS

Merton came to understand leaving the world in terms of withdrawing from it to gain a better perspective of its truth, reality, demands, and limitations. He knew that his increasingly physically isolated living situation only enhanced the ability he had to speak prophetically—and that he did. Pieties remained essential to his own spiritual practice, but such private expressions of faith could no longer be an end-all for him. As he wrote in a letter to a Jewish friend in January 1961:

> Too often today the idea of "hope" is presented in a totally untheological and secular form, as a kind of pious optimism that "everything will be all right," presumably because it is the nature of things to be all right. But as we know, it is not exactly the nature of things to be all right, since man has a way of following his sinful will in strange directions, and causes have effects.[14]

Another book published in 1966 (he was urgently writing, then, as usual) attempted to do in verse what he was doing in prose essays in those other books—and in magazines. In *Raids on the Unspeakable*, he attacks problems as a modern-day prophet would. Race. Anti-Semitism. Poverty. War. All these issues consumed him, as his life deepened, to the point where he felt them intensely and felt that he had to speak out against them with all his influence. People would listen to the famous Thomas Merton, and they did.

He was bitter at times, ironic at others, in these prose poems. Both the prophetic essays and the poems were like weapons of words. Their meaning wasn't always precise ("Is he talking about the war in Vietnam?" "Is that a reference to racial hatred?")—but it was powerful and pointed. The world was clearly something that Merton was sure-footed in and that most people were floating unconsciously through.

For example, the Voting Rights Act was being bitterly debated when Merton wrote what is in *Raids on the Unspeakable*. The Vietnam War was being turned up by the Johnson administration. There was a war on poverty. The Second Vatican Council was wrapping up. To those who would use Jesus as an excuse to be pious and not care about the enormous problems, Merton wrote:

> *Into this world, this demented inn, in which there is absolutely no room for Him at all, Christ has come uninvited. But because He cannot be at home in it, because He is out of place in it, His place is with those others for whom there is no room.*[15]

The wilderness in which Merton was living was not simply geographical or situational. He knew that—like the original desert, wilderness, and forest hermits—he needed distance from the world to properly understand and interpret it. This was his vocation: to pray and write, and he prayed and wrote most often in his last years about the world and its problems. There are people who are called to live in the middle of troubles, and pray and minister there, and then there are those called to live a distance apart from where the troubles are occurring, to pray and understand them from there. That was Merton's calling.

He began to critique being comfortably white, middle class, and Christian—sixty-plus years ago—in ways that have become more accepted and realized since that time. He wrote,

for example, long before the rest of us began to catch on that
Christendom was falling down:

> *Indeed, the concept of a "Christian society" is one that needs
> to be clarified today. Certainly the affluent, secularized society
> of modern Europe and America has ceased to be genuinely
> Christian. Yet in this society Christians tend cling to vestiges
> of their own tradition which still survive, and because of
> these vestiges they believe they are still living in a Christian
> world. . . . It is unfortunately true that Christians themselves,
> for one reason or another, may in the name of God himself
> and of his truth, cling to subtle forms of prejudice, inertia, and
> mental paralysis.*[16]

One reason, I believe, why we still look to Merton today for
wisdom on world events—fighting racial hatred, protesting war,
nonviolent resistance, opposing religious prejudice—is because
he articulated the issues in his time in ways that are still relevant. Also, there is an authenticity about his life and teachings
that is felt beneath the surface of the writings themselves. His
writing flowed effortlessly and organically out of his life. I'm
sure readers can sense this. For example, it was the day after
Thich Nhat Hanh visited him at Gethsemani, in spring 1966,
when Merton wrote the beautiful reflection entitled "Nhat Hanh
Is My Brother"—and just as quickly he sent it off to the editor
at *Jubilee,* who published it in the August 1 issue of the magazine.[17]

MAKE LIFE A COMPOSITION

This is why Merton sought to live in the hermitage: to pray better, and differently, in ways that had become impossible for him in the monastery. He wrote to a Sufi friend:

> *Strictly speaking I have a very simple way of prayer. It is centered entirely on attention to the presence of God and to His will and His love . . . it is a matter of adoring Him as invisible and infinitely beyond our comprehension and realizing Him as all.*[18]

It is, in light of this, that one can best understand his poetry—which we haven't discussed much—and his photography and drawings, which were also a deeply personal expression of his middle-aged life. A photograph is a picture of what the photographer sees. Merton's poems, too, functioned this way.

In his early years, the poems were full of monastic and religious imagery. The later poems are rich with tension, ambivalence, and sometimes fury. To read them is to experience a writer who is living very much in the world—has, in fact, taken the concerns of the world onto the shoulders of his pen. (See "Suggestions for Further Reading" for recommendations of where to start.)

Whether it was writing or visual art, there simply are those whose vocation is to leave traces for others to follow. We follow Merton—and by that I mean we are drawn to him and what he has to say—because we can intuitively sense that authenticity.

He was one of those rare religious people who are both idealistic and generous. Most religious people have the idealism pounded out of them. "Get real!" people say, even to monks in a monastery.

Another simple reason we love him is that he had the unusual quality of being a priest willing and able to be honest about his problems. Merton's problems were often obvious, sometimes less noticeable, but always he was open in sharing them. This is one of the reasons why so much of his writing is memoir and autobiography; he wants to share what he has learned and is learning, and the learning is in real time.

He admitted early on, in *The Sign of Jonas,* a memoir that the censors of his religious order almost didn't allow him to publish: "The truth is I am far from being the monk or the cleric that I ought to be. My life is a great mess."[19] That may be so, but in that mess each of us who understands our life also as a kind of pilgrimage may find direction. As Merton showed, a monk can be anyone who seeks God, is being found by God, and is willing to give themselves to the search for what is true, beautiful, lasting, and loving in this world of ours. In those things, and through Merton's life, teachings, and spiritual practices, we might experience God.

Suggestions for Further Reading

In my view, Merton's most important books (excluding poetry) in the order in which they were published:

The Seven Storey Mountain (1948)

Seeds of Contemplation (1949)—later revised as *New Seeds of Contemplation* (1962)

The Sign of Jonas (1953)

No Man Is an Island (1955)

The Way of Chuang Tzu (1965)—this was his favorite of his books

Conjectures of a Guilty Bystander (1966)

Zen and the Birds of Appetite (1968)

All the letters—You may want to begin with the one-volume compilation:

A Life in Letters: The Essential Collection, eds. William H. Shannon and Christine M. Bochen. Notre Dame, IN: Ave Maria Press, 2010.

All the journals—You might want to begin with this one-volume
    compendium:
    The Intimate Merton: His Life from His Journals, eds. Patrick Hart
        and Jonathan Montaldo. New York: HarperCollins, 2001.

For the poetry, start here:
Emblems of a Season of Fury. This is my favorite. Published in
    1963, it comprises shorter poems, including many prose po-
    ems. They reflect the wide and expanded range of Merton's
    concerns, addressing political situations, recent tragedies,
    contemplative life, and the natural world.
Then, don't miss these individual poems from other volumes:
    "Trappists, Working" (written early in his monastic life)
    "Chant to be used in Processions around a site with Fur-
        naces" (discussed above)
    "Hagia Sophia" (a longer poem, on wisdom and the femi-
        nine, quoted above)
    "Evening"
You can find each of these in *In the Dark before Dawn: New Se-
    lected Poems*, ed. Lynn R. Szabo. New York: New Directions,
    2005; and *The Collected Poems of Thomas Merton*. New York:
    New Directions, 1980.

For the photographs and drawings, start here:
Paul M. Pearson, ed., *Beholding Paradise: The Photographs of
    Thomas Merton*. New York: Paulist Press, 2020.
Thomas Merton, *Dialogues with Silence: Prayers and Drawings*, ed.
    Jonathan Montaldo. New York: HarperOne, 2004.

John Howard Griffin, *A Hidden Wholeness: The Visual World of Thomas Merton*. Boston: Houghton Mifflin, 1979.

Good single-volume collections of his writings:

A Thomas Merton Reader: Revised Edition, by Thomas Merton, ed. Thomas P. McDonnell. New York: Image, 1974. This was the standard work for decades. It unfortunately lacks an index.

A Book of Hours, by Thomas Merton, ed. Kathleen Deignan. Notre Dame, IN: Sorin Books, 2007. Short writings organized for use as prayers throughout the day.

For his teachings on mysticism to the young monks:

A Course in Christian Mysticism: Thirteen Sessions with the Famous Trappist Monk, by Thomas Merton, ed. Jon M. Sweeney. Collegeville, MN: Liturgical Press, 2017.

Six excellent books about Merton:

James Finley, *Merton's Palace of Nowhere: 40th Anniversary Edition*. Notre Dame, IN: Ave Maria Press, 2018. A personal, wise introduction to Merton's spiritual vision, written by a former spiritual directee under Merton as a monk at Gethsemani, who then left and became a trained psychotherapist and profound spiritual teacher in his own right.

James Martin, SJ, *Becoming Who You Are: Insights on the True Self from Thomas Merton and Other Saints*. Mahwah, NJ: Hidden Spring, 2005. By one of the most popular Catholic spiritual writers since Merton, this book is both warm and profoundly practical.

Michael Mott, *The Seven Mountains of Thomas Merton*. Boston: Houghton, Mifflin, 1984. Still the most comprehensive biography. Now out of print.

Christopher Pramuk, *Sophia: The Hidden Christ of Thomas Merton*. Collegeville, MN: Liturgical Press, 2015. For those who enjoy reading theology, this is probably the best book ever written on Merton's mystical theology, focusing on how he was drawn to Wisdom.

William H. Shannon, *Silent Lamp: The Thomas Merton Story*. New York: Crossroad, 1993. For most readers, this is the most useful biography of Merton, because the author understands monasticism—its demands, rewards, and challenges. Now out of print.

Paul Wilkes (ed.), *Merton By Those Who Knew Him Best*. New York: Harper & Row, 1984. Short essays by important people who knew and loved Merton. Now out of print.

Acknowledgments

This book has been a long time coming. I've been preoccupied with Merton since high school. I mentioned in the introduction my flirting with monastic life at Gethsemani. When I married at twenty-one, I even took along Monica Furlong's biography of the monk on my honeymoon. When I was in seminary at twenty-two and twenty-three, I began to write. My first published essay came out at that time, in a small academic journal, comparing the ideas of John Hick and Hans Küng on interfaith dialogue (a preoccupation of Merton's). I also, at that time, published two poems in *The Merton Seasonal,* which was then edited by the great, now late, Robert Daggy.

Thank you to Joel Fotinos for the invitation to write the book. Thank you to Professor Michael Murphy of Loyola University Chicago for an invitation to give a paper on Merton the writer at the Catholic Imagination Conference in 2019. Thanks also to Fr. John Mack of Buffalo, from whom a warm invitation to speak about Merton the writer and mystic at Christ the King Seminary came in while I was writing. Preparing those presentations helped me form nascent ideas into clearer ones.

Notes

Simple Chronology

1 William H. Shannon, ed., *The Hidden Ground of Love: The Letters of Thomas Merton on Religious Experience and Social Concerns* (New York: Farrar, Straus and Giroux, 1985), 561.

Introduction

1 James Martin, SJ, "Becoming Who We Are," in *What I Am Living For: Lessons from the Life and Writings of Thomas Merton,* ed. Jon M. Sweeney (Notre Dame, IN: Ave Maria Press, 2018), 4.

2 Stephen Spender, as quoted in introduction to *World Within World* (New York: Modern Library, 2001), vi.

3 *No Man Is an Island* (New York: Dell, 1957), 126.

4 Robert Inchausti, in *Soul Searching: The Journey of Thomas Merton,* ed. Morgan Atkinson and Jonathan Montaldo (Collegeville, MN: Liturgical Press, 2008), 190.

1. He's Finally Free

1 Thomas Merton, *The Asian Journal of Thomas Merton,* ed. Naomi Burton, Patrick Hart, and James Laughlin (New York: New Directions, 1975), 338.

2 Fenton Johnson, "Going It Alone: The Dignity and Challenge of Solitude," April 2015, *Harper's,* 10.

2. A World-Weary Man

1 Thomas Merton, *The Seven Storey Mountain: Fiftieth Anniversary Edition* (New York: Harvest/Harcourt, 1998), 49.

2 William H. Shannon, ed., *The Hidden Ground of Love: The Letters of Thomas Merton on Religious Experience and Social Concerns* (New York: Farrar, Straus and Giroux, 1985), 605.

3 Merton, *The Seven Storey Mountain,* 123.

4 Ibid., 78.

5 Jim Knight, "The Thomas Merton We Knew," published online 1998, http://www.therealmerton.com/index.html.

6 Edward Rice, *The Man in the Sycamore Tree: The Good Times and Hard Life of Thomas Merton* (Garden City, NY: Doubleday, 1970), 25.

7 In an interview with William Shannon. William H. Shannon, *Silent Lamp: The Thomas Merton Story* (New York: Crossroad, 1993), 105.

8 Arthur W. Biddle, ed., *When Prophecy Still Had a Voice: The Letters of Thomas Merton and Robert Lax* (Lexington: University Press of Kentucky, 2001), 45.

9 Merton, *The Seven Storey Mountain,* 320.

3. Finding What He Was Looking For

1 Thomas Merton, *The Seven Storey Mountain: Fiftieth Anniversary Edition* (New York: Harvest/Harcourt, 1998), 410.

2 Thomas Merton, *A Course in Desert Spirituality: Fifteen Sessions with the Famous Trappist Monk,* ed. Jon M. Sweeney (Collegeville, MN: Liturgical Press, 2019), 147.

3 Brother Paul Quenon, OCSO, interview with Judith Valente, "Religion & Ethics Newsweekly," PBS, June 4, 2009, https://www.pbs.org/wnet /religionandethics/2009/06/04/june-5-2009-brother-paul-quenon-on -thomas-merton/1392/

4 Merton, *A Course in Desert Spirituality,* 148.

5 Thomas Merton, *The Secular Journal* (Garden City, NY: Image Books, 1969), 167.

6 "Religion: White Man's Culture," *Time,* November 29, 1948, http://content .time.com/time/magazine/article/0,9171,804927,00.html.

7 Patrick Samway, SJ, ed., *The Letters of Robert Giroux and Thomas Merton* (Notre Dame, IN: University of Notre Dame Press, 2015), 33.

8 Thomas Merton, *Bread in the Wilderness* (New York: New Directions, 1997), 107.

9 See "An Argument—of the Passion of Christ," in Thomas Merton, *A Man in the Divided Sea* (Norfolk, CT: New Directions, 1946). The opening line of the review of this book in *America* magazine went: "Out of the quiet of a Trappist monastery has come one of the most authoritative poetic voices of our time."

10 "chicken instead of a duck": Thomas Merton, *The Sign of Jonas* (New York: Harvest, 1981), 89; "It was he who": Ibid., 90.

11 Ibid., 3.

12 Thomas Merton, *Entering the Silence: The Journals of Thomas Merton, Vol. 2 (1942–1952)*, ed. Jonathan Montaldo (New York: HarperCollins, 1997), 398.

13 See ibid., 389.

14 Ibid., 400.

15 Randall De Trinis, "A Novice and His Master," *The Merton Seasonal* 34 (2009): 15–17.

16 Thomas Merton, *No Man Is an Island* (New York: Dell, 1957), 12, 78.

17 Thomas Merton, *Conjectures of a Guilty Bystander* (New York: Doubleday, 1966), 49.

18 Merton expert William H. Shannon identifies the turning point year for this maturation as 1958. If you're interested in more about this, see chapter 10, "Return to the World, 1958," in William Shannon, *Silent Lamp: The Thomas Merton Story* (New York: Crossroad, 1993), 178–91.

19 Printing and pricing information on *Seeds of Contemplation* obtained from advertisement at the back of a first printing edition of Merton, *No Man Is an Island.*

20 Thomas Merton, *New Seeds of Contemplation* (New York: New Directions, 2007), 180.

21 Merton, *The Sign of Jonas*, 13.

4. In a Furnace of Ambivalence

1 C. C. Abbott, ed., *The Letters of Gerard Manley Hopkins to Robert Bridges,* (New York: Oxford University Press, 1955), 157.

2 All three sentences are from Thomas Merton, *New Seeds of Contemplation* (New York: New Directions, 2007), 34.

3 Bruce Foltz, ed., *Medieval Philosophy: A Multicultural Reader* (New York: Bloomsbury Academic, 2019), 164.

4 Thomas Merton, *The Sign of Jonas* (New York: Harvest, 1981), 4.

5 Ibid., 5.

6 James Laughlin, from "Thomas Merton: A Portrait," in David D. Cooper, ed., *Thomas Merton and James Laughlin: Selected Letters* (New York: W. W. Norton, 1997), 379.

7 Letter of February 8, 1948, in ibid., 30.

8 Letter to Rabindranath Tagore, Chinmoy Guha, ed. and trans., *Bridging East and West: Rabindranath Tagore and Romain Rolland Correspondence (1919– 1940)* (New Delhi: Oxford University Press, 2018), 12.

9 Fred Bahnson, "On the Road with Thomas Merton," *Emergence Magazine,* 2019, 105.

10 Merton, *New Seeds of Contemplation,* 260.

11 Merton, *The Sign of Jonas,* 222.

12 See Richard Loomis in Paul Wilkes, ed., *Merton by Those Who Knew Him Best* (New York: Harper & Row, 1984), 135–39.

13 Merton, *The Sign of Jonas,* 9.

14 To Dom Gabriel Sortais, Patrick Hart, ed., *The School of Charity: The Letters of Thomas Merton on Religious Renewal and Spiritual Direction* (New York: Farrar, Straus and Giroux, 1990), 101.

15 Br. Benet Tvedten, OSB, *How to Be a Monastic Without Leaving Your Day Job: A Guide for Benedictine Oblates and Other Christians Who Follow the Monastic Way* (Brewster, MA: Paraclete Press, 2013), 89.

16 James Finley, *Merton's Palace of Nowhere: 40th Anniversary Edition* (Notre Dame, IN: Ave Maria Press, 2017), 53.

17 Thomas Merton, *Contemplative Prayer* (New York: Image, 1971), 19.

5. Needing Intimacy and Love

1 Aldous Huxley, *Ends and Means: An Enquiry into the Nature of Ideals* (London: Chatto & Windus, 1946), 7–8.

2 Merton quote: Thomas Merton, *Conjectures of a Guilty Bystander* (New York: Doubleday, 1966), 144. Cardinals disagreeing: see Archbishop Carlo Maria Viganò arguing with Pope Francis's efforts at dialogue and interreligious exchange from November 2019, "Letter #62, 2019: Viganò on the Danger of Syncretism," Inside the Vatican, https://insidethevatican.com /news/newsflash/letter-62-2019-vigano-on-the-danger-of-syncretism/.

3 Thomas Merton, *The Behavior of Titans* (New York: New Directions, 1961), 76.

4 Paul Kingsnorth, *Savage Gods* (Columbus, OH: Two Dollar Radio, 2019), 38.

5 Thomas Merton, *Zen and the Birds of Appetite* (New York: New Directions, 1968), 7.

6 This poem is titled "Untitled Poem" and was published in the rare volume, Thomas Merton, *Eighteen Poems* (New York: New Directions, 1985).
It's rare because only 250 copies were printed, and the book has never
been reprinted. These poems have been called Merton's love poems, or
sensuous poems.

7 Thomas Merton, *The Seven Storey Mountain: Fiftieth Anniversary Edition*
(New York: Harvest/Harcourt, 1998), 383.

8 William Shannon, *Silent Lamp: The Thomas Merton Story* (New York: Crossroad, 1993), 200.

9 Joan Baez in Paul Wilkes, ed., *Merton by Those Who Knew Him Best* (New
York: Harper & Row, 1984), 42.

10 Christine M. Bochen, ed., *Learning to Love: The Journals of Thomas Merton,*
vol. 6 (New York: HarperCollins, 1998), 66.

11 William H. Shannon, ed., *The Hidden Ground of Love: The Letters of Thomas
Merton on Religious Experience and Social Concerns* (New York: Farrar, Straus
and Giroux, 1985), 157.

12 Doug Burton-Christie, "Rediscovering Love's World: Thomas Merton's
Love Poems and the Language of Ecstasy," *Cross Currents* 39 (Spring 1989):
65.

13 Thomas Merton, *Turning Toward the World: The Journals of Thomas Merton,* vol. 4, ed. Victor A. Kramer (New York: HarperCollins, 1997), 17; and
Thomas Merton, *Emblems of a Season of Fury* (New York: New Directions,
1963), 61.

14 Thomas Merton, *New Seeds of Contemplation* (New York: New Directions,
2007), 26.

15 "Love and Need: Is Love a Package or a Message?" in Naomi Burton Stone
and Patrick Hart, eds., *Love and Living* (New York: Mariner Books, 2002),
26–27.

6. Moving Toward Wholeness

1 Thomas Merton, *Conjectures of a Guilty Bystander* (New York: Doubleday,
1966), 153.

2 Ibid., 154–55.

3 I thank Marjorie Corbman for making me aware of these points. She did
so in her talk, "'Welcome, Brother Merton': The Challenge of the Black
Power Movement to Thomas Merton's Thought on Non-Violence," a paper delivered at the International Thomas Merton Society's 16th General
Meeting, June 27–30, 2019, Santa Clara, California.

4   Letter to Jean Leclercq; see Patrick Hart, ed., *The School of Charity: The Letters of Thomas Merton on Religious Renewal and Spiritual Direction* (New York: Farrar, Straus and Giroux, 1990), 95.

5   Thomas Merton, *The Wisdom of the Desert* (New York: New Directions, 1960), 3.

6   Thomas Merton, *The Seven Storey Mountain: Fiftieth Anniversary Edition* (New York: Harvest/Harcourt, 1998), 188.

7   Thomas Merton, *The Other Side of the Mountain: The Journals of Thomas Merton*, vol. 7, ed. Patrick Hart, OCSO (New York: HarperCollins, 1999), 205. For the Vietnam War as motivation for Merton to go to Bangkok, see his journal entries from March 12 and 14, 1968.

8   Thomas Merton, *The Way of Chuang Tzu* (New York: New Directions, 1997), 12.

9   Thomas Merton, *The Asian Journal of Thomas Merton*, ed. Naomi Burton, Patrick Hart, and James Laughlin (New York: New Directions, 1975), 236.

7. Creating Monastic Spirituality for Everyone

1   Thomas Merton, *Contemplative Prayer* (New York: Image, 1971), 19.

2   Thomas Merton, *The Silent Life* (New York: Farrar, Straus and Cudahy, 1957), 166–67.

3   Thomas Merton, *Conjectures of a Guilty Bystander* (New York: Doubleday, 1966), 154.

4   Br. Benet Tvedten, OSB, *How to Be a Monastic and Not Leave Your Day Job* (Brewster, MA: Paraclete Press, 2006), 103.

5   Mary Gordon, *On Thomas Merton* (Boulder, CO: Shambhala, 2019), 50.

6   See, for instance, Thomas Merton, *The Asian Journal of Thomas Merton*, ed. Naomi Burton, Patrick Hart, and James Laughlin (New York: New Directions, 1975), 341. I'm paraphrasing.

7   Paul Quenon, OCSO, *In Praise of the Useless Life: A Monk's Memoir* (Notre Dame, IN: Ave Maria Press, 2018), 1.

8   Thomas Merton, "Is the World a Problem?" *Commonweal* 84, no. 11 (1966).

9   Merton, *Conjectures of a Guilty Bystander*, 12.

10 Thomas Merton, *Disputed Questions* (New York: Harvest, 1985), 186.

11 From Christine Valters Paintner, *Illuminating the Way: Embracing the Wisdom of Monks and Mystics* (Notre Dame, IN: Ave Maria Press, 2016), quoted by Paintner on her blog on "the feast day of Thomas Merton," his death date, under the heading, "Thomas Merton and Embracing Your In-

ner Monk," Abbey of the Arts, https://abbeyofthearts.com/blog/2015/12
/06/thomas-merton-and-embracing-your-inner-monk-a-love-note-from
-your-online-abbess/.

12 Richard Rohr, *The Universal Christ: How a Forgotten Reality Can Change Everything We See, Hope for, and Believe* (New York: Convergent, 2019), 241, 37.

13 Merton, *Conjectures of a Guilty Bystander,* 309.

14 Thomas Merton, *New Seeds of Contemplation* (New York: New Directions, 2007), 15.

15 William H. Shannon, ed., *The Hidden Ground of Love: The Letters of Thomas Merton on Religious Experience and Social Concerns* (New York: Farrar, Straus and Giroux, 1985), 136.

16 Ibid., 70.

17 Ibid., 265.

18 *Seeds of Destruction* (New York: Farrar, Straus and Giroux, 1964), 33.

19 Eldridge Cleaver, *Soul on Ice* (New York: McGraw-Hill, 1968), 52–55.

20 William Shannon, *Silent Lamp: The Thomas Merton Story* (New York: Crossroad, 1993), 198.

21 Joan Baez in Paul Wilkes, ed., *Merton by Those Who Knew Him Best* (New York: Harper & Row, 1984), 41.

22 See William H. Shannon, ed., *Witness to Freedom: The Letters of Thomas Merton in Times of Crisis* (New York: Harvest, 1995), 226–30.

8. Leaving Sainthood Behind

1 Thomas Merton, *Disputed Questions* (New York: Harvest, 1985), 207.

2 William H. Shannon, ed., *The Hidden Ground of Love: The Letters of Thomas Merton on Religious Experience and Social Concerns* (New York: Farrar, Straus and Giroux, 1985), 157.

3 Sister Thérèse Lentfoehr, *Words and Silence: On the Poetry of Thomas Merton* (New York: New Directions, 1979), 43.

4 Thomas Merton, *Cold War Letters,* ed. Christine M. Bochen and William H. Shannon (Maryknoll, NY: Orbis, 2006), 10.

5 Luce and her husband, Henry Luce (publisher of *Time* magazine), gave Gethsemani the three thousand acres in South Carolina that became a daughter house, Our Lady of Mepkin Abbey, in 1949. See Michael Mott, *The Seven Mountains of Thomas Merton* (Boston: Houghton Mifflin, 1984), 254.

6 James W. Douglass, foreword, in Merton, *Cold War Letters,* xii–xiv.

7   James Martin, SJ, "The Belly of a Paradox: Forty Years After His Death, Thomas Merton Still Causes Controversy," BustedHalo.com, December 10, 2008, https://bustedhalo.com/features/the-belly-of-a-paradox.

8   Thomas Merton, *The Other Side of the Mountain: The Journals of Thomas Merton,* vol. 7, ed. Patrick Hart, OCSO (New York: HarperCollins, 1999), 75–76.

9   Thomas Merton, *The Asian Journal of Thomas Merton,* ed. Naomi Burton, Patrick Hart, and James Laughlin (New York: New Directions, 1975), 24–25.

10 Thomas Merton, *The Way of Chuang Tzu* (New York: New Directions, 1997), 10.

11 Fons Vitae, http://www.fonsvitae.com.

12 Thich Nhat Hanh in Paul Wilkes, ed., *Merton by Those Who Knew Him Best* (New York: Harper & Row, 1984), 151.

13 Jonathan Montaldo, ed., *Dialogues with Silence: Prayers and Drawings* (New York: HarperOne, 2004), xi.

14 Thomas Merton, *Conjectures of a Guilty Bystander* (New York: Doubleday, 1966), 158.

15 Thomas Merton, *Run to the Mountain: The Story of a Vocation: The Journals of Thomas Merton, Vol. 1 (1939–1941),* ed. Patrick Hart, OCSO (New York: HarperCollins, 1996), 458. Entry from November 28, 1941.

16 Robert Giroux remembered these words of Merton's. See Patrick Samway, SJ, ed., *The Letters of Robert Giroux and Thomas Merton* (Notre Dame, IN: University of Notre Dame Press, 2015), 10.

17 These two letters are from David D. Cooper, ed., *Thomas Merton and James Laughlin: Selected Letters* (New York: W. W. Norton, 1997), 35, 38.

9. We Are All Secrets

1   Thomas Merton, *The Other Side of the Mountain: The Journals of Thomas Merton,* vol. 7, ed. Patrick Hart, OCSO (New York: HarperCollins, 1999), 147–48.

2   From a talk at the Naropa Institute in 1983, recorded in *The Chronicles,* an online journal. "On Meeting Thomas Merton," *Chronicles,* April 19, 2019, https://www.chronicleproject.com/christian-buddhist-dialogue/.

3   Quoted in William H. Shannon, *Silent Lamp: The Thomas Merton Story* (New York: Crossroad, 1993), 206.

4   Thomas Merton, *The Asian Journal of Thomas Merton,* ed. Naomi Burton, Patrick Hart, and James Laughlin (New York: New Directions, 1975), 107.

5   Patrick Samway, SJ, ed., *The Letters of Robert Giroux and Thomas Merton* (Notre Dame, IN: University of Notre Dame Press, 2015), 15.

6   Raimundo Panikkar, *Blessed Simplicity: The Monk as Universal Archetype* (New York: Seabury, 1982), 92 and 8.

7   Thomas Merton, *The Silent Life* (New York: Farrar, Straus and Cudahy, 1957), vii.

8   Merton, *The Other Side of the Mountain,* 80.

9   Merton, *The Silent Life,* 131.

10 Julius Lester, "Contemplation in a World of Action (Review)," *New York Times,* March 14, 1971, 34.

11 Thomas Merton, *The Seven Storey Mountain: Fiftieth Anniversary Edition* (New York: Harvest/Harcourt, 1998), 346.

12 Ibid., 352.

13 Merton, *The Asian Journal,* xxix.

14 To Rabbi Zalman Schachter-Shalomi; William H. Shannon, ed., *The Hidden Ground of Love: The Letters of Thomas Merton on Religious Experience and Social Concerns* (New York: Farrar, Straus and Giroux, 1985), 533.

15 Thomas Merton, *Raids on the Unspeakable* (New York: New Directions, 1966), x.

16 Thomas Merton, *Life and Holiness* (New York: Herder and Herder, 1963), 54–55.

17 Shannon, *Silent Lamp,* 201.

18 Shannon, *The Hidden Ground of Love,* 63–64.

19 Thomas Merton, *The Sign of Jonas* (New York: Harvest, 1981), 193.

ABOUT THE AUTHOR

JON M. SWEENEY is an independent scholar and an award-winning writer. He is a biographer of St. Francis of Assisi and translator of his writings, and his books on Franciscan subjects have sold more than two hundred thousand copies. Jon is the author of more than forty books, including *The Pope Who Quit*, which was optioned by HBO. He is editor in chief and publisher of Paraclete Press. He's appeared on *CBS Saturday Morning* and numerous other programs, and writes regularly for *America* magazine in the United States, and *The Tablet* in the United Kingdom. Jon is married to Rabbi Michal Woll; their interfaith marriage has been profiled in national media. He's the father of four, and lives in Milwaukee.